A special message to all Discovery employees
from the dirty guy on the cover...

Hello friends! Mike Rowe here, *Dirty Jobs*, et cetera.

In your hands is a special edition of my mother's hilarious new book *About Your Father and Other Celebrities I Have Known*.

What makes this special edition so special? Well, aside from this special message from me to you . . . not much.

The stories herein are identical to those in the original edition, as is the cover design, the foreword, the afterword, the acknowledgements, and the dedication. The only real difference is the page you're reading now, which I've added for the express purpose of thanking David Zaslav. Shortly after the national lockdown, David invited me to speak during a virtual townhall for Discovery employees, and in the course of my remarks, I shamelessly plugged my mother's latest book, thereby inspiring David to purchase a thousand copies on the spot.

Those of you who know David will not be surprised by his generosity or his spontaneity. Those of you who know me will not be surprised by my suggestion that he immediately increase his purchase to five thousand copies.

"David," I said, "I'm so grateful for this, and my mother will be thrilled, but if you order five thousand copies, the publisher can call it a 'special edition,' which means I can write something honest and heartfelt directly to your employees. What do you say?"

David, no doubt sympathetic to the challenges of marketing a book at a time when all of the bookstores are closed (or perhaps worried that I'd never stop negotiating with him), agreed to purchase the additional copies, which is why you are now the proud owner of a very funny book published at the height of a global pandemic written by an 82-year-old woman you've probably never heard of.

On the other hand, perhaps you have?

Peggy Rowe's first book, *About My Mother*, was written at the age of 80 and went on to become a *New York Times* bestseller. My mom writes only about things that interest her and does so in a style she finds personally amusing. In other words, she doesn't try to please anyone but herself, which I think is precisely why she's found success as a writer.

For that matter, I think it's also why Discovery has found success as a company. As for my father, the subject of this book, I'll discuss him in the Foreword, which you'll find in the following pages. I'd rather use the final paragraphs in this "special edition" to simply say how honored I am to be a part of your family.

I started with Discovery in 1993 as the cohost of something called *Romantic Escapes,* a well-intended but doomed travelogue that required me to create the illusion of romance in five-star resorts all over the world. It was a pretty good gig but proved conclusively that you can't always judge a show by its title. *Romantic Escapes* was canceled after 13 episodes, but I stuck around for the next ten years, mostly as a narrator, and slowly worked my way up to the sewer on a little show called *Dirty Jobs.* Since *Dirty Jobs* debuted in 2004, not a week has gone by where I haven't appeared in some way, shape, or form on one of the many channels in the Discovery family of networks.

I'm very proud to have had such a great run with Discovery, and very fortunate to be a part of this ever-growing family. Now, my mother would like to introduce you to her family—specifically to the man she's lived with for the last sixty years. A man who still watches every rerun of *Dirty Jobs* and still yells at the screen whenever he sees me doing something he doesn't like. In this way, I imagine my father has something in common with David, whom I'd once again like to sincerely thank for buying my mom's new book in such copious quantities, and for passing one on to you.

Please enjoy it in good health. And see you on TV.

Mike Rowe
Dirty Jobs, et cetera

P.S. By "et cetera," I refer not only to *Deadliest Catch, After the Catch, Bering Sea Gold, How the Universe Works, How Booze Built America* ,and various other projects I've done for Discovery, but also to my own *New York Times* bestselling book, *The Way I Heard It,* which I'm confident David will one day purchase in equal quantity . . . .

ABOUT YOUR FATHER

→ AND OTHER CELEBRITIES I HAVE KNOWN ←

*Ruminations and Revelations from a
Desperate Mother to Her Dirty Son*

Peggy Rowe

Forefront
BOOKS

About Your Father
And Other Celebrities I Have Known

Ruminations and Revelations from a Desperate Mother to Her Dirty Son

Published by Forefront Books.

Cover Design by Bruce Gore, Gore Studio Inc.
Interior Design by Bill Kersey, KerseyGraphics

ISBN: 978-1-948-67737-0
ISBN: 978-1-948-67745-5 (eBook)

→ DEDICATION ←

*To our three sons: Mike, Scott, and Phil, who continue
to be my inspiration. You will undoubtedly recognize and
appreciate this man I have portrayed with love and humor.
Thanks for being such an integral part of our lives and for
making the occasional cameo appearance in this book.*

⇸ ACKNOWLEDGMENTS ⇷

THANKS TO FRIEND, EDITOR, AND WRITER Michele "Wojo" Wojciechowski who was the first to read these stories. When you laughed out loud, I knew they were good enough to share. I appreciate your great suggestions.

Thanks to Lisa Stilwell who edited my manuscript with a fine-tooth comb and with kindness. You made it look like a real book, Lisa. You really are great at what you do!

Where would I be without the loyal staff at MRW Productions who are there for me every day of the week? I so appreciate your help, Mary, Jade, Chuck, Shari, Lara, Libby, and Melanie. You are like family!

Thank you, Forefront Books and Jonathan Merkh—publisher, friend, taskmaster, and hand holder-in-chief. Let's do this again someday.

To son Mike Rowe who clearly doesn't understand the concept of old age and retirement. Thanks for always being there, Mike. You make work seem like fun.

→ TABLE OF CONTENTS ←

Foreword. 11

Any Day Now. 17

Home Sweet Stable. 21

High Hopes 29

The Energy Czar. 33

Tough-ish Love 39

Four Degrees of Separation—and Counting. 45

It Must Be Magic 49

Party Animals—Not. 55

Red, White, and Brown: The Price of Celebrity 61

The Rapture. 67

Mother Love. 71

Happy Birthday, Firstborn 77

About Face 81

On Being a Mother 85

Elevator Man 91

What's a Wife for, Anyway? 95

It's All in the Wrist 99

The Family Table 103

By the Seat of His Pants 107

Old Blue 115

What's a Mother to Do? 121

We're Keeping Him 127

Poo-Dini 131

Old Blue—The Follow-Up 135

Imposters in Tinseltown 139

Family Celebs 149

Something to Chew On 159

On Familiar Ground: Romancing the Garbage 163

The Long Ride Home 169

The Doctor Is In 173

The Old Gray Pair 179

Time to Come Clean! 183

Afternoon Delight 189

The Auto Train 191

The Good Times 195

Family—A Mixed Blessing 199

My Traveling Man 203

A Perfect Storm 209

The Fabric of Life 211

Not Our Turn 215

The Wandering Recluse 221

Material Man 225

Afterword by John Rowe 227

Important People: My LFBF 229

⇝ FOREWORD ⇜

SEVERAL YEARS AGO, MY PARENTS BEGAN receiving checks in the mail for seemingly random amounts of money. The checks arrived every week and prompted dozens of concerned phone calls from my father.

"Hello?"

"Michael. It happened again."

"Hi Dad. What happened again?"

"The checks. We got two more today. One for me. One for your mother."

"Hey, that's great!" I said. "Money for nothing, chicks for free!"

"What?"

"Never mind," I said. "It's a line from a song."

"What's going on here, Michael? Why do these people keep sending us money?"

"Because you earned it, Dad. Welcome to the world of advertising."

"But we already did the work. We've already been paid. I didn't agree to any of this . . . extra money."

"It's not 'extra money.' It's a residual check. Enjoy it!"

My father sighed. He and my mother had filmed some commercials with me for Viva paper towels several months before. Neither had expected to be paid. They looked at the whole experience as a field trip—a chance to hang out in Hollywood with their oldest son and maybe run into some celebrities. Now these unexpected paychecks were generating questions.

"Why are they always for different amounts? This is the third week in a row, and the amounts are never the same. Something's wrong here."

"Nothing's wrong, Dad. Some weeks the commercials air more than others. The more they air, the more you make."

"Well . . . how long do these Viva people plan on airing these commercials?"

"I don't know. Maybe a year? Maybe more?"

"Maybe? What do you mean, maybe? How am I supposed to plan for the future if these Viva people keep sending me money whenever they feel like it? And what about all these withholdings? What does 'R-SAG CONTR' mean? Or 'CASDI?' Do you have any idea how much tax California takes? Good grief, Michael, what have you gotten me into?"

Reread that last paragraph, and you'll begin to understand the essence of John Rowe. Only a man like my father can refuse to cash a paycheck he doesn't believe he's earned, while agonizing over deductions he doesn't believe he owes. This is the man my mother has lived with for sixty years. A man she still calls her "Prince Charming" (with varying degrees of irony). A meticulous man who provided for a family of five on a schoolteacher's salary. A passionate man who worked in community theater for fifty years, purely for the joy of it. A frugal man who, to this day, will spend an hour online taking a McDonald's survey in order to get a code that gets him a free Quarter Pounder when he buys one at the regular price. This is the man you're about to meet. This is my father.

I remember the day we filmed that Viva commercial in Los Angeles. The goal was to demonstrate that Viva paper towels—in spite of their festive name—were tougher than the competition. *"Tough, even when wet!"* That was the message the agency wanted to impart, so I proposed a very personal approach, with a campaign called "Pigpen Comes Home." In the spot, I would arrive at my parent's house—fresh from a *Dirty Jobs* shoot—covered in grime. From their living room, Mom and Dad would see me walking up their driveway and arm themselves with rolls of Viva paper towels. Then they'd follow me around their house, wiping off everything I touched while engaging in witty banter. Clever, right?

My mother writes about this day in great detail, because the Viva commercial shoot was the beginning of her great Hollywood adventure. But Mom left out a few details. She neglected, for instance, to mention that the photo on the cover of this book was taken that very same day. In between takes, I had asked the photographer to get a shot of my parents posing as the stoic farmers in Grant Wood's iconic painting, "American Gothic."

"Why?" said my father. "What does 'American Gothic' have to do with selling paper towels?"

"Nothing, Dad. But we have a professional photographer on hand and a pitchfork. Besides, you never know when a photograph like this might come in handy." My father frowned, the way he always does he finds my explanations lacking.

"What's my motivation?" he asked.

"Your what?"

"You know, my motivation. What's driving my character? What sort of expression should I have on my face?"

"The look on your face right now is perfect," I said.

My father sighed some more and shook his head, as my mother assumed an equally dour expression. "Who knows, John, maybe this will be the cover of a book one day?"

My father snorted. "A book? Who's going to buy a book with us on the cover?"

It was a reasonable question. Back in 2012, my eighty-year-old father had no way of knowing his seventy-five-year-old wife was destined to become a bestselling author. In those days, she was just another aspiring writer, sending her oldest son an ever-growing collection of stories, letters, emails, and texts. During the Viva shoot, I recall her scribbling feverishly on yellow legal pads. She scribbled in her trailer, she scribbled during lunch, she scribbled on the set. Little did I know, her scribblings would turn into two books. And little did my father know, he'd wind up on the cover of this one, holding a pitchfork and staring solemnly into the camera, looking very much like the man he is. A man with questions.

It makes little sense to talk too much about my father here, since my mother has devoted the next 225 pages to doing that very thing, but I want to share another moment she neglected to include from that fateful day. It was a small moment, but one that I treasure. We were shooting the first setup—a scene in the backyard—and the Viva people were nervous. They had approved the concept for "Pigpen Comes Home," but they hadn't realized that I would insist on casting my real parents.

"Do your parents have any experience?" the director asked me.

"Oh yes," I told him. "They've been playing my parents for over fifty years."

"No, I mean do they have any experience acting in commercials?"

"Nope. None whatsoever."

"Well, then, with respect," he said, "how do I know they can act?"

"With respect," I replied, "you don't. But my Dad's done local theater for decades, and my mother has a wicked sense of humor. Trust me; they'll be fine."

Anyway, the scene in the backyard involves me eating spare-ribs at a picnic table while my father cleans off a greasy grill in the background. Three cameras cover the action as my mother swoops in, says something charming, and then wipes some BBQ sauce off my face with a Viva towel. My mother is subtle in real life, so her demeanor and mannerisms are perfect for television. She nails it in one take, and everyone breathed a sigh of relief.

Then my father lifts up the towel he's been using to clean the grill with and casually says, "These Viva towels really *are* tough—even when wet."

Except, that's not what happened.

Unlike my mother, my father is *not* known for subtlety; he is known for clarity. And though his work on the stage has been well-received, fifty years of community theater had not prepared him for the kind of understated nuance the director was expecting. This was made apparent when my father whirled around from the grill with great gusto, face aflame with wonder and excitement. In his hands, he gripped a greasy Viva paper towel, which he held aloft in much the same way Hamlet might present the skull of poor Yorick. Then, like a Shakespearean actor addressing the back row of a sold-out theater, my dad looked directly into the camera and boldly delivered his one and only line, while tugging on the wet towel:

"HOLY SMOKES! THESE VIVA PAPER TOWELS REALLY *ARE* TOUGH . . . *EVEN WHEN WET!!!*

Unfortunately, the Viva tore in half the second he tugged on it, just as any wet paper towel would under such an enthusiastic assault. Of greater concern, however, were the eardrums of those huddled around a giant monitor twenty feet away watching the scene unfold. The director, the producer, and the clients were all wearing headsets when my father's booming voice sent them flying up and out of their chairs. Some screamed in alarm and threw their headsets across the room, while others gripped their chests and fell to the floor. In the stunned silence that followed, my Dad tossed the shredded towel onto the grill and said, "Cut! Nice job, everyone. That's a wrap!"

By the fourth take, my dad reeled things in a bit, and delivered a highly nuanced, beautifully understated performance. Consequently, my parents and I were invited to film a number of additional spots for Viva, which triggered more of those pesky residual checks, which my father ultimately justified cashing by dramatically increasing his year-end charitable giving. He still has questions about all those mysterious withholdings and abbreviations, but, by and large, he's let it go. As for my mother, she can still be spotted in her local grocery store autographing rolls of Viva paper towels for her many fans. Even though the residuals have dried up, she continues to sing their praises, as does my father, who takes great pleasure in wringing them out, letting them dry, and then using them again. Old habits die hard, I suppose.

Anyway, that's a long way of telling you that my mother has done it again. *About Your Father* is a terrific collection of funny stories about a devoted husband, written by a woman uniquely qualified to tackle the task at hand. Like her first book, this one is really a love letter to the man she refers to as her "Prince Charming." A man who, after reading the book you've just begun, called me from Baltimore to say that the stories in this collection are among the finest he's ever read. In fact, his exact words to me were, "You know, Michael, I do believe this is the kind of book that could be enjoyed by just about anyone . . . *EVEN WHEN WET!!!*"

I'm pretty sure they heard him in Hollywood.

Mike

→ ANY DAY NOW ←

IN NOVEMBER OF 1960, I SAID, "I DO," AND moved out of my parents' comfortable home. I was twenty-two, and I'd never written a check—unless you count the one I gave the man at the college bookstore where all I had to do was fill in the amount. I'd never shopped or cooked or ironed. I grew up with parents who simply indulged my obsession with horses. Mom was queen of her domestic domain and happy not to have me underfoot. On my wedding day, she warned my husband to be patient. "I'm afraid Peggy doesn't know much about housekeeping," she told him.

John, on the other hand, was twenty-eight and had been on his own since his late teens—including a stint in the US Army, a job with the US Postal Service, and four years at college. He had purchased automobiles, arranged for housing, managed a bank account, and taken care of his everyday needs. Oh yeah, John Rowe knew a thing or two about survival and economy. My husband was a minimalist. His life was about thrift and getting by on a shoestring with no frills—just the bare necessities.

Marriage was culture shock for both of us, and 1961 was a killer. Moving out of my parents' home and into a second-floor apartment that didn't have a television, radio, telephone, or washing machine (not that I had ever used one) was like moving to a Third World country. There was a new word in my vocabulary that year: *budget.*

For John, a wife who expected to purchase a new outfit just because it was Easter—when there were clothes already hanging in her closet—and then had the nerve to make the unreasonable request of "Let's get a telephone"—when there was a perfectly good telephone downstairs in the landlord's living room—well, let's just say that the new word in John's vocabulary was *extravagant.*

I had taught school for a whole year, but my husband insisted that we save my salary. "After all," he said, "we'll have to live on one salary when we have a family. We may as well get used to it."

That we survived our first year is testament to the fact that I loved this weird man I had married, despite his extreme frugality. And he was devoted to the indulged young woman who had grown up in the "lap of luxury."

Thanks to intimacy—which came more naturally than cooking and cleaning and was more or less free—our marriage not only survived, it prospered and increased.

I was five months pregnant on our first anniversary and looked forward to a modest celebration at the Double T Diner, where we ate most Friday evenings after work. It was our only luxury and preceded the weekly grocery shopping, which cost us a whopping $15.

But on November 19, my frugal husband said something that caused me to pass out right there on the floor. "Put your new dress on, hon. We're having dinner at the Candlelight Lodge!"

Now, the Candlelight Lodge was absurdly expensive, and as I've said, the concept of *splurging* was as commonplace in our home as pole dancing in our church sanctuary.

"We're what? You know they're expensive, right? And it's Saturday. They'll probably be crowded."

"I made reservations. Come on! We're going out on the town!"

If my husband was feeling celebratory, who was I to argue? There was a lot to celebrate, after all. Our careers were progressing nicely, our first child was due in the spring, and I had finally gotten past the horrendous morning sickness, which was a cruel misnomer as it had lasted all day long—for four months.

So I put on my beautiful new maternity outfit—an early Christmas gift. The expensive aqua satin sheen material had been purchased by my sister and sewn by my mother on her old Singer treadle sewing machine.

I felt like Cinderella as we were escorted to our candlelit table by a man in a tuxedo, who, thanks to his exaggerated posture, resembled the figure atop a fancy bottle stopper my father had received as a gift. There was tasteful piano music in the background—a Strauss waltz, I believe—that made me think of my mother. I would be sure to include that detail when I called her tomorrow (on the telephone in the landlord's living room).

"Is everything okay?" I asked minutes later after John picked up the menu and every bit of color drained from his face. Even in the flickering candlelight he was the color of our new percale sheets.

"It's fine! We're celebrating!" he said, forcing a smile. We both ordered the surf and turf and exclaimed over every morsel. One of us might have observed that, considering the cost, the portions seemed modest—in comparison to the Double T, where we always left carrying a doggie bag. We had even ordered one small glass of white wine. It was a time before the world had been enlightened about the effects of alcohol on pregnancy, and I had a few sips with dinner. We discussed baby names over our crème brûlée and coffee. If it was a boy, it would be Michael, which was John's middle name. The evening was definitely picture worthy, and in current times, I would have snapped selfies with my cell phone.

We left holding hands and headed for our car. I probably looked up at the moon and said, "I will remember this magical evening forever, hon," because it's the sort of thing I say.

It was in the parking lot just before we reached our car that the magic gave way to that old feeling—nausea. I heaved—and lost my crème brûlée. I heaved some more and lost my surf and turf. I didn't actually lose it, as there were globs on my new aqua maternity outfit, as well as on my husband's freshly shined shoes . . . and the front bumper of his beloved old Dodge. Again, it might have been a perfect cell phone moment.

John was no stranger to hurling. It had been part of our daily routine for the past four months. Sometimes I even awoke in the middle of the night to run to the bathroom and gag. Early on, John had shown great compassion, standing beside me, holding my hair away from my face, or gently stroking my back, then getting me a drink. In more recent months, he was more about getting out of my way—and out of earshot.

Now, on a lovely Saturday evening in the restaurant parking lot, my husband appeared to be in a state of shock, rallying just enough to run back inside for some paper towels. This was one detail that would not make it into my call to Mother the next day. To his credit, not once did John complain that I had just thrown up a meal that cost more than our weekly food budget. And he waited until we were almost home before marveling aloud that the same person who could keep down a Double T greasy burger, fries, and crab dip, should have trouble with tenderloin and crab imperial.

Not that my husband would ever hold a grudge. But it was a long time before he would splurge on a five-star meal again.

It could happen any day now.

⇥ HOME SWEET STABLE ⇤

*B*EFORE WE WERE MARRIED, JOHN TOLD ME right up front: "I have never cared for horses, and I doubt that I ever will." He said this knowing of my lifelong passion for horses—preferring them to people, in some cases. So, naturally, I told him that I thought history was boring—a subject for which he had equal passion.

John's statement about horses didn't really bother me, because I was confident I could turn him around. Help him to see the light, so to speak. I had three friends who were doing that very thing with their own boyfriends, and in one case, husband.

One of my friends had fallen for a guy who was known to have an affinity for other men. It bothered her, but she was confident that the love of a good woman would change him. They married in college.

Another friend married a man who had been a philanderer—even fathering children out of wedlock. She had no doubt that true love and marriage would change his reckless ways.

Then there was Connie, who was fully aware of Harold's drinking. But she was sure that all he needed in his life was a good wife, and all would be well.

The day John agreed to climb onto a horse and accompany me on a trail ride, I knew that my optimism and patience had paid off.

"Old Shaker is a perfect beginner horse," I had told him. "I taught my mother to ride on Old Shaker. And Mom's in her *forties*! You're going to love Old Shaker!"

"Huh," he grunted. I took this as a positive *huh*. John was not an effusive person, after all. The gushiest I had ever seen him was over my mother's pot roast—and the pie she'd made from the apples in our orchard. Even then his praise was restrained—though he had seconds of each.

I had been giving riding lessons for several years, and my beginning students were ordinarily introduced to horses in the schooling ring. I decided on a different approach for John. Riding in circles is tedious for adults, especially men, and I wanted him to be wowed from the start. So I gave him a quick tutorial—just some rudimentary commands—"where the brakes and accelerator are, and how to operate the steering mechanism," as he put it. I complimented him on mounting so effortlessly.

He shrugged and said it was merely a matter of overcoming gravity. Then we began our peaceful ride through the cool, shady woods—the first of many, hopefully, with squirrels and rabbits scampering across the ground and birds chirping in trees. Bonding on horseback—me on Jet, and John on Shaker—over the occasional sighting of a deer, or groundhog, or fox. Really! It couldn't get much better than that. My boyfriend was going to get hooked on horses if I had anything to do with it!

I didn't bother alerting John to the annoying spider webs strung across the trails that smacked the lead rider in the face. They were my concern. I plucked a small branch with leaves to swat the air in front of my face as we rode along.

I try not to spend my time in useless speculation, but I have often wondered if things would have turned out differently had I remembered to warn John of low-hanging branches—the kind that sweep you off your saddle like a kitchen broom in the hands of my efficient, determined mother.

I was a first-rate tour guide that day, pointing out the exposed roots of a fallen tree, now home to a family of foxes; a large round hole high in the trunk of a poplar where flying squirrels sometimes appeared and sailed through the air; and the open, bare, spot on the trail where I had seen a black snake sunning himself.

So far, so good. He was loving it! I could tell! It was heavenly, riding along in companionable silence, just the way I had dreamed. I turned around in the saddle to talk about the approaching stream where water cascaded over an impressive formation of rocks. I wasn't ready for the sight that greeted me. Nothing was there.

Way back on the trail, Shaker was riderless and jogging in my direction. Alongside him was John, looking for all the world like he was on a pogo stick. With his left foot in the stirrup, he bounced up and down along the trail on his right foot—holding onto the saddle for dear life and yelling, "Whoa, dammit!"

When Shaker reached us, he stopped, and with one final hop, John pulled himself into the saddle.

"Why did you get off?" I sputtered. "I didn't show you how to dismount."

"Technically speaking, I didn't *get* off," he said, in a less than enthusiastic tone. "*Old Shaker* swerved off the trail. Then *Old Shaker* took me under a low branch. *And I think he did it on purpose!*"

"Are you sure? He's never done anything like that before."

"Really? Well, it was a first for me too!" He started brushing dried leaves and pine needles from his shirt.

"Oh, well," I said, "we'll just chalk it up to gravity." I resisted the urge to call him Hopalong. Maybe someday it would seem funny.

Despite John's ominous introduction to horses, he seemed in good spirits as we finished our ride. He even walked bowlegged to his car—where he reached inside and took out what looked like a history textbook. "Here you go," he said. "I brought you a little thankyou gift."

I don't remember the title—or the author. Only that it was about two inches thick with fine print and no pictures, and I didn't read a word of it.

That was the first and last time John rode a horse. That said, horses would intrude on his life for years to come. And for the most part, my husband was an amazingly good sport about that intrusion. That said, there were times . . .

——≫-◆-≪——

Three years and one child into our marriage, we bought a house that was bordered by a field, woods, and a stream. Eight years later, John and my father built a four-stall stable and fenced in a pasture. Because our three young sons insisted on having a pony. (All right, that's an outright lie. We all know the truth. A horse addiction, like any other, is almost impossible to shake.)

Had John known the ramifications of being a horse owner, he might have objected vigorously.

No matter how hard I tried to keep my obsession in check, there was a wee bit of overlap into my domestic life.

Like that morning when John was running late for work and called from the bathroom, "Where's the radio, hon?"

"Oh, I listened to it in the stable yesterday while we soaped saddles; sorry."

I could hear his sigh from the kitchen.

"I don't have time for the paper in the morning. I'd at least like to hear some news while I'm shaving . . . and why does it smell like horses in here?"

I reached into the bathroom and quickly grabbed the stable towels from behind the door, shoved them down the laundry chute, and sprayed some air freshener. I made a mental note to bring the radio back into the house, along with the alcohol and Vaseline I'd used to treat a scrape on the pony's shoulder.

Minutes later, John hurried into the kitchen half-dressed and opened a drawer. "Where are the scissors? They should be right here in this drawer!"

"Oops," I said. "We braided Cindy's mane the other day. I must have left them in the tack room." I lifted the lid from a pot on the stove. "Look, hon, your favorite breakfast! Bran mash—I mean, oatmeal with raisins." I was probably remembering last week when I had fixed a pot of bran mash with apples and carrots for the animals. I was in the basement putting in a load of wash when five-year-old Scott ran to me in tears.

"Mommy, Nana's here. She started stirring the bran mash, and before I could stop her, she ate a spoonful. You tell us not to eat the horse's molasses feed because it'll make us sick. Is Nana going to die?"

I assured our son that nobody was going to die or even be sick. He took it better than my mother, who said something about my priorities. I don't think it was a compliment.

I thought back to the day before when I had inadvertently dialed the veterinarian's number to make an appointment for our son's check-up. It was funny at the time, but that was one little piece of humor I wouldn't be sharing.

"Maybe we should just move into the stable. Half of our stuff is already there." John looked down at his bare legs, frowned, and pointed toward the bedroom. "My pants had better be hanging in that closet."

"Don't be absurd," I said. "The horses' legs are too short for your pants." Men don't have much of a sense of humor before breakfast.

When John and the two older boys were seated at the table, I looked around and asked where three-year-old Phil was.

"Maybe you left him in the barn," my husband suggested.

I might have chuckled, just a little. "He was here a minute ago," at which point Phil popped out from under the table.

"I'm not hungry, Mommy. Can I go to the stable and play with my toys?"

John shook his head and rolled his eyes. Fortunately, he left for work by way of the back door on this particular morning and didn't go through the living room where I had plopped a freshly soaped saddle over the back of his favorite chair.

As I've said, there were some isolated occasions when my horse obsession might have filtered into our domestic lives, but I was generally careful. The day my husband returned from work to find a bathroom sink full of soaking snaffle bits, I had baked a cake, and the house was filled with his favorite aroma—meatloaf encrusted with brown sugar and catsup, accompanied by new potatoes and baby carrots.

"It will be out of the oven in ten minutes, hon," I said, rinsing the bits and scooping them from the sink.

Through the years, when the topic of horses came up, John's favorite comment was, "Oh, yeah. When we got married, the minister said to me, 'John, do you promise to take this woman—these two horses, and this dog?' " It always gets a laugh. I guess I owe him that.

After we had our first child, my husband and I were in no position to keep a horse, so after much soul-searching, I had found a good home for my beloved Jet. The Humane Society of Baltimore County had a large farm where a small herd of horses received loving care. The managers offered to keep Jet until I was ready to take him back. We visited him through the years, but it was that first visit months later that has remained with me to this day.

The herd was in the stable finishing their evening meal when we arrived. When Jet looked up and whinnied softly to me, I simply lost it. The tears in John's eyes said it all—you don't have to share your spouse's passion to appreciate it.

"I felt so sorry for you," he told me later. "I think that was the moment I first realized just how deeply you loved that horse."

John continues to be a good sport about my horse obsession. Whether we're chasing after wild ponies on Assateague Island, following the fox hunt in northern Baltimore County, visiting the Baltimore City police horses, or standing on the sidelines at a polo match or horse show, I'm sure of one thing: my husband is always there for me—looking up from his book from time to time and smiling.

Not all of us are quite so fortunate in life. Like my three college friends, for instance, who thought, mistakenly, that they could change the men they loved. I think back to John's words all those years ago. "I've never cared for horses, and I doubt that I ever will." It's funny, the things we do for love.

→ HIGH HOPES ←

Hi Mike,

Sorry to bother you, but I need to tell you what happened yesterday. On a grand scale it's probably nothing, but, well, let's just say that your father is still recovering. I would appreciate your worldly take.

Compared to most people, we've led quiet lives and have a reputation for being straightlaced. It's a distinction well earned. If there is one thing your father has zero tolerance for, it is breaking the law. His rap sheet includes an overdue library book, jaywalking (twice that I can remember), and a parking fine (he misread the meter). As for me, I was stopped by a policeman for a burned-out taillight sixty-one years ago (I was eighteen). I'm sure you'll agree that all of our infractions have been unremarkable.

When our old friend and neighbor died two years ago, his widow went to live with their daughter, Regina, in New Mexico. Regina has always appeared to be a loving, devoted daughter. She was in town for a wedding this week, so we invited her to lunch—along with another neighbor, Jim, who had also been close to the family.

Regina, as usual, was in high spirits—bubbly and friendly, entertaining us with stories of her "flower child" days. She's sixty-two.

"When I was at school, there were four groups of people. The straight kids—like you guys," she said looking at Jim and Dad and me with a tolerant smile, "and the heads, the juicers, and the druggies."

I told her there were three groups of people back when I was in school: academic, commercial, and general. She smiled again.

Regina didn't elaborate on which group she had belonged to, but I'm guessing it wasn't the first one. Not that we would ever be judgmental, either way. After all, that was forty some years ago— long before she became a responsible adult.

"And how is your mother doing?" Dad asked. "We want to hear all about Maggie."

"Oh, Mom's great since I started her on marijuana three times a day," she said, reaching out and scooping up some veggie dip with a whole grain cracker as calmly as if she had just said she'd started her mother on cranberry grape juice three times a day.

Iced tea came bubbling out of your father's nose. "What?!" he exclaimed, wiping his chin, then reaching up to make sure he had remembered to put in his hearing aids that morning.

"Marijuana," Regina repeated calmly. When there was no response, she spoke louder. "Marijuana!" she bellowed, like she was talking to a roomful of elderly deaf people.

I have to tell you, Mike, I was glad the windows were closed.

"It's good for her memory, and she doesn't fall down as often."

Jim and your father sat there staring with their mouths open as though they'd been anesthetized for a medical procedure. You know how your father shakes his foot when he's tense? Well, all of a sudden it was going like a metronome on steroids while the tips of his laces made little click, click, click sounds against his foot brace.

"I'm pretty sure that's illegal!" Jim said, as we sat there picturing our ninety-year-old friend, Maggie, lighting up a joint.

"Not to mention dangerous!" added your father. I knew what he was thinking—that Maggie had stopped falling because Maggie had stopped walking.

"No, no, Mom gets the cannabinoids—CBDs. They're not

psychoactive. Don't worry, she's not going to be arrested—I got her a medical marijuana card. She eats three chocolate candies a day. You should try it. It's great for older people. They call it brain food."

Seconds passed in silence . . . well, except for the click, click, click of Dad's shoelaces. Naturally your father was the one who asked the question all three of us were thinking—the elephant-in-the-room question.

"Um, so, do you use marijuana too?"

"Sure, I do," she said, flicking the long hair from her eyes. "I have been for years. I like a hit first thing in the morning." She made it sound perfectly normal—like your father reading the paper and having a biscotti with his morning coffee.

Click, click, click.

"It's gets me going. Wake and bake they call it," she said while laughing. Jim and I forced a laugh, but Dad looked comatose, except for the appendage at the end of his left leg.

Click, click, click.

"Then, about five hours later, I light up again—THC this time. That's more potent. But I don't get stoned . . . at least not during the day."

Dad dabbed iced tea from his chin as his whole chair vibrated making little creaking sounds, while Jim stared. Honestly, I didn't know what to think, Mike. I've always associated marijuana with criminals, but Regina says I'd be surprised how many professionals use it. I tried to picture my Dr. Lisa lighting up a joint. I guess our shock was obvious.

"Weed gets a bad rap," she said waving her hand. "But it's good for depression, anxiety, insomnia, pain." She sounded like a spokesman for the recreational marijuana industry testifying before Congress.

"I'm telling you, Mom is better off today than when she came to me. She's still forgetful, but she doesn't care. She's a lot more mellow."

It occurred to me that I might have benefitted from some weed when I was caring for your grandmother. Especially that day she stood up from her wheelchair and stripped off her blouse in the main aisle of Macy's department store. Between you and me, I could have used a couple of those little chocolate delights right there on the spot. Or that day she ran over me with her Rascal Scooter. I could have used a half dozen or so of those beauties.

"So, do you have a bunch of stock in the cannabis industry?" your father asked her.

"No," Regina laughed. "But I do have some growing in the back-yard. They call it "molta" in Spanish. The potent part is the bud; that'll get you high in no time. Sometimes I smoke to get relaxed; sometimes I smoke to get motivated. Like I tell my husband, 'It's for molta-va-tion.'" I laughed along with her, but Jim and your father looked as though they had just witnessed a bludgeoning.

Honestly, Mike, I don't know what to think. It felt like Cannabis 101, and by the time she finished talking, I didn't know whether to call the cops or place an order.

On her way out, Regina put her hands on her hips and gave a short public service announcement: "Remember—a bud a day keeps a stroke away."

I followed her to the elevator where I spoke earnestly.

"Regina, you don't drive when you're smoking, do you?"

"Heavens no!" she said as though the idea were preposterous. "I'd get pulled over for going ten miles an hour."

Your father thinks Regina was messing with us, but I've been doing a little research. Did you know that glaucoma patients can legally purchase cannabis? Not that I ever would! Although it seems a shame to go through life never even trying something. I'm just saying.

Love you,
Mom

P.S. We had a small glass of red wine with dinner last evening. Your father says that makes us juicers. Does it, Mike?

⇢ THE ENERGY CZAR ⇠

*F*OLLOWING A BLOG POST I WROTE ABOUT MY husband walking in the neighborhood after dark—in the rain—I received some interesting comments. They ranged from heartfelt concern to criticism. Some even accused John of a selfish disregard for the drivers who might run into him, throw him onto the hood of their car, and frighten them.

There were also helpful suggestions. Some readers told him to wear reflective clothing so that he can be seen. Others said he should carry a flashlight. When several people told me I should buy him a headlamp like the ones miners wear, I had to laugh. I know my husband, and I could see my future. In no time, he would have us both wearing headlamps in a dark house.

"Hey hon," he'd say. "These little babies are perfect! We're lighting up only the parts of the house we really need to see. We're not wasting electricity in areas we're not using."

So typical! My husband has been flicking off light switches as long as I've known him. It was his full-time job when the kids were at home, following them from room to room like they were the Pied Piper.

"There's nobody in this room," he'd say. *Click!* "Why are these lights on?" *Click!*

If they complained, "But, Dad, I'm coming right back," he'd say, "When you're paying the electric bill, you can leave as many lights on as you want." *Click!*

More than once, I yelled, "Hey! I'm in here!"

"Well, you've lived in this house long enough to know your way around in the dark," John would say, laughing and turning the light back on.

They say it's darkest before the dawn, but in our house, it was darkest after my husband got home from work. "Hey," he'd say, walking through the door, "This house is lit up like New Orleans during Mardi Gras. Astronauts can see our house from space."

Click! Click! Click!

The day my husband took the almost empty toothpaste tube to the basement and put it in the workbench vise to squeeze out the last drop, the kids were fascinated. I told them that this would be our little family secret. When he washed used aluminum foil and smoothed it out for reuse, I explained that their father was poor growing up and hated waste.

From time to time, John was able to laugh at himself. Like the day we took the kids to the Maryland Science Center. For four hours we saw fascinating exhibits, demonstrations, and films. When it was time to leave, he checked the parking meter.

"There is no way I'm leaving twenty-five minutes on that meter," he said. "Come on guys, we're taking a hike around the harbor." I said I was exhausted and would sooner wait in the car for twenty-five minutes, thank you. When the tired kids piled in behind me, John chuckled, got behind the wheel, and started the engine.

<hr />

Nothing revealed John's thrifty nature—or impacted our lives—quite like the new addition in our home. Taking up residence on the fireplace hearth at the far end of the kitchen and weighing in at 650 pounds, the black steel Warner woodstove became not only the focal point in our lives, but the center of our winter world. It was made by John's brother, Robert, a master welder, and as such, had great sentimental value.

The decision to purchase the woodstove followed daily news coverage of the impending increase in oil prices over the coming months.

"Now we can turn off the furnace and heat the house with wood. There's a forest full of fuel out back," John announced, pointing toward the picture window and the woods beyond, "and all the cheap labor we need," he said, looking over his glasses at three healthy sons.

Nothing achieved family participation quite like the woodstove. Not even Monopoly, Sorry!, or 500 Rummy. From gathering logs, splitting, and stacking them, to feeding the stove's insatiable appetite and shoveling out the ashes, there were plenty of chores to go around.

My husband was like a child on Christmas morning those first few weeks. With the new woodstove roaring, he walked through the house morning and night holding a thermometer high in the air with one hand and carrying a notebook in the other. In each room, he paused to record times and temperatures.

"Peg, light a candle and come upstairs with me," he said late one frigid January night. "I want to see if the heat's getting up there."

"John, we'll wake the kids."

"Nah, come on." He led the way up the steps while holding the thermometer high, with me following close behind with a candle—looking for all the world like a religious procession on a high holy day.

"Brrr, it's freezing up here," I whispered. "Look, Michael's wearing his coat in bed! John! Is the child even breathing?"

"Well, of course he's breathing. You can see his breath." He pointed to the little puffs of white cumulus clouds coming from our son's nostrils. It was only a matter of time until Child Protective Services would come knocking at our door.

Suddenly Mike's eyes popped open, and he bolted upright. "Wh . . . what are you guys doing?"

"Just taking some readings, son. Go back to sleep."

"Geez, Dad, I thought you were the Statue of Liberty! Is that you, Mom? Don't drip candle wax on my homework. The teacher already thinks we don't have electricity. She told me twice I smell like a wood fire. You didn't turn off the electricity, did you?"

"Go back to sleep, son."

John checked the thermometer and made notes in his book. Downstairs, while I topped off the water in the heavy black iron pot on the stove, he checked our little weather station, then recorded the temperature, humidity, and air pressure on a chart on the refrigerator door.

"It's too dry," he said, shaking his head. "We have to be sure to keep that pot filled with water! *And* we need to install a fan in the wall to get more heat upstairs."

The following morning, my husband was at it again. "Listen to this, Scott," he said as our son came down the steps wrapped in a blanket. "It was 70 degrees in the kitchen and 65 degrees in the living room at 7:00 a.m. At 7:00 p.m. last night, it was 81 degrees in the kitchen and 73 degrees in the living room. How about that?

"Well it's 32 degrees upstairs, and my nose hairs are frozen stiffer than icicles. How about that!" Scott said.

"That's why they make blankets," John told him.

"The dog slept on top of me, and I was still cold," Scott replied.

"Hmm," John said, winking at me. "Maybe it's time to get another dog, hon."

Scott's brother came down the stairs behind him. "Hey, the toilet bowl looks like a skating pond, Dad. Is it okay to flush?"

"No, Phil," Scott said. "We'll have to wait for the spring thaw."

John says the children have inherited my penchant for sarcasm. Just for the record: no one in our family experienced frostbite during those years.

"Scott, it's your turn to shovel some ashes from the stove," John said.

"All right, but you might be getting a note from the teacher. She thinks I smoke."

"And Phil, you run up to the woodpile. Take the wheelbarrow with you."

"I feel like Daniel Boone," Phil muttered, putting a coat on over his Dungeons and Dragons jacket and heading for the door.

Scott left for school that day prematurely gray with singed eyebrows.

———

The Warner stove was our primary heat source for the next ten years. During that time, John reached a level of proficiency that would have qualified him to teach Woodstove 101 at the local community college, had there been such a course. If woodstove had been a national sport, my husband would surely have medaled. Sadly, our woodstove was ahead of its time. It would have been great material for a certain reality show on, say, The Discovery Channel.

⇢ TOUGH-ISH LOVE ⇠

*J*T WAS SUNDAY MORNING, AND I LOOKED OUT at the congregation as my quartet played the final note of the prelude. We were strictly amateur, mind you. A piano, a violin, a guitar, and my recorder. (Our church is desperate for music in the summer while the choir is on vacation.)

From the third pew, my youngest son, Phil, grinned—or maybe it was a giggle. Mike gave me a thumbs-up, Scott put his fingers to his lips in a mock whistle, and my teenaged granddaughters waved, as though they weren't embarrassed in the least. It was déjà vu, except for one small detail. This time, I was the one at the front of the room performing—not my children or grandchildren. My family had come full circle, and it was gratifying.

Later, still in the afterglow of performing for my family (and to the glory of God, naturally), I commented to my husband, "Raising three sons was the most rewarding experience of my life. Don't you wish we could turn back the clock and do it all again?"

John lowered his paper and stared at me as though my eyebrows had ignited.

"Have you lost your mind?!"

His response didn't surprise me. Our children are products of two distinct styles of parenting. Though our goals were the same, my husband and I often disagreed on how to achieve them. Most of the time, John deferred to my child-rearing skills. I had come from a secure, happy family, after all—think of *Leave It to Beaver* and *Father Knows Best*. That said, there were occasions when this father stood firm and held his ground. In the tradition of my own parents, (and June and Ward Cleaver), our disagreements took place behind closed doors, so that our children grew up believing that their parents were always of one mind. Imagine!

Lobbing a friend's stink bomb into the classroom of the most unpopular teacher in junior high school was out of character for Michael. But there he was, an eighth grader walking down the hall with a friend, when he did the unexpected. Bedlam ensued, and for the first time in his school career, our son saw the inside of the principal's office.

What transpired next is the way I remember it. Mike has since written a slightly different narrative, which is the way he remembers it. The basic facts are in agreement.

I knew something was wrong that afternoon when he sat quietly at the kitchen table, his head in his hands.

"I did something really stupid today. I've never done anything this bad in my whole life. How could I be so dumb?"

I hadn't seen Mike this dejected since we initiated the "no TV on school nights" policy. "Whatever it is, it can't be all that bad," I said, giving him a reassuring hug then sliding the cookie jar toward him. "Tell me about it."

He finished his tale of woe with words I never expected to hear from one of my children.

"I'm suspended for three days."

My jaw dropped. Suspension was a big deal, especially in this family of educators. But naturally, I couldn't scold the boy—not in his distraught state.

"After three days, you have to come for a conference with the vice principal," he added, giving me a sideways glance. "Mr. Smith is a terrible teacher. He makes fun of kids in front of the whole class—especially Joey when he stutters. He actually mimics him.

Did I mention that it was a smoke bomb too?" He covered his face with his hands.

"Michael," I said, putting my arm around him. "I'm going to tell you a story about your grandfather. I think it will make you feel better."

To the extent that any mortal being can achieve perfection in this life, my father had. Years later, Michael would eulogize him, using words such as humble, honest, generous, forgiving, and brilliant. Quite simply, Carl Knobel embodied the qualities people most admire and aspire to.

"When Poppie was your age, he smoked cigarettes, and one day he got caught smoking in the outhouse at Fullerton School." Michael lifted his head.

"What? Poppie?"

"Uh-huh. He left school that day with a note for his parents. They had to come in for a conference before their son could return. He hid the note, and for the next three days, instead of going to school, your grandfather camped out at the stream until it was time to go home."

"Our stream? Stemmers Run?"

"The very same. After three days of hiding out and fretting, he came clean—to his mother. So, she went in for a conference, and all was forgiven."

"Poppie did that?" Michael said, reaching for a cookie. He seemed to be adjusting to his predicament.

I thought that three days of homework would be ample punishment. More importantly, it would give students and teachers time to forget the unfortunate incident.

The final hurdle Michael now had to face was driving up the lane in the family station wagon as we spoke.

As a teacher, John was horrified and not in the least interested in Mr. Smith's shortcomings as an educator. As a father, he agreed with his son—his behavior had been stupid. Our son was inconsolable that evening, so John said nothing in the way of admonishment. The following morning, he rose early and told Michael to get ready for school.

"I'm not allowed to go for three days, remember? I don't want to go to school today."

"You are going back today!" insisted his father in a tone that meant *no arguing*! "Staying home for three days is out of the question!"

I protested—privately, of course, comparing my husband to Abraham in the Old Testament. "You're sacrificing our son to the education gods!" I declared, in an absurd, dramatic plea that made even me smile.

John rolled his eyes and stood firm. In the vice principal's office, he pled his son's spotless record. "He's ashamed and regrets his actions, and wasting three days at home is absurd."

The administrator relented, and Michael faced the music that day while I sat at home imagining my poor boy the object of ridicule and rejection. As an adult, Mike made a startling confession. The stroke of luck we now refer to as The Stink Bomb Incident had elevated his status among his peers—from measly, shy eighth grader to that of conquering hero.

"It was the best thing that could happen to a shy kid in junior high school," he now admits. "All the kids hated that teacher. Hiring a publicist couldn't have done what that stink bomb did for me." Our son had slain the dragon!

John swears that Mike's self-loathing that afternoon was a stroke of premeditated genius. To this day, whenever we admire one of his public appearances, John shakes his head and says, "Of course, it can't compare to the stink bomb performance!"

——◆——

The next time my husband stood his ground was when Michael was an Eagle Scout candidate, and John insisted he pay his own way for a week at Philmont Scout Camp in Arizona.

"But it's a worthwhile activity," I argued. "He should go, and we should pay for it."

"He'll appreciate it more if he earns it," insisted John. I relented, and for the next year, our son saved every cent he made cutting grass, shoveling snow, chopping wood, and washing cars. He would later describe Philmont as one of the most enriching experiences of his youth.

When it was time for college, John insisted that Mike should be responsible for buying his own books.

"That's unreasonable!" I argued. "We've saved for this. We can afford it!"

"He has a part-time job, and he's a good student," insisted John. "The responsibility will be good for him. Let's just see if he can do it."

He could. And he did.

Our strongest disagreement came after Mike graduated from college and decided to continue his telemarketing job and live at home. John actually charged his own son rent.

"He's our son, for goodness sake! We can't take his money!" I said.

"He'll have to pay rent when he leaves," John argued. "Let's just see if he can do it."

He could. And he did.

On the day Mike finally moved out of our home, John presented him with the savings account into which he had deposited the cost of the Philmont trip, and his college text books, and his rent for two years.

To this day, Mike thanks his father for his tough-ish love.

FOUR DEGREES OF
→SEPARATION—AND COUNTING ←

$\mathcal{J}$T WAS THE YEAR OF MY HUSBAND'S FIERCE summer cold. He had the works, all right: sore throat, cough, congestion, and swollen glands. He thought he was at death's door. I know this because he resorted to the unthinkable. He paid a visit to our Dr. Lisa, who prescribed antibiotics along with a mega dose of advice—as usual.

"You are contagious, John! Stay away from Peggy!" she warned. "No hugging! No kissing! No touching! Don't even look at her!"

I shook my head when he came home and told me. "I have to deliver a speech next week and a eulogy the following week. I cannot, under any circumstances, catch your cold."

"Okay," he said. "No kissing . . . no hugging."

"And I'd better sleep in the guest room for now," I said.

I could tell my husband was devastated when I came from the bathroom and gathered up my nightgown, slippers, and robe. Poor thing lay alone and forlorn on his side of our comfortable, queen-size, pillow-top mattress with a summer-weight embroidered bedspread—the one my mother had made for us. We had shared a bed for over fifty years, and now . . .

"I'll see you at breakfast, hon," I said, brushing the hair from his forehead, lingering just long enough to see if he had a fever.

He did not. "Everything you need is right here on the bedside table," I said. "Including your cell phone. Call if you need me. Love you."

Our guest room is smaller than the master bedroom, with a comfortable queen-size bed and private bath. There's a radio and a reading lamp—neither of which I used. We all have our creature comfort requirements, and mine include a quiet, darkened room in order to fall asleep. If I use the overhead fan at all, it has to be on low. John is not as particular but has graciously acquiesced to my needs over the years.

And so it went. My husband going to bed alone, quietly, with cough syrup, tissues, antibiotics, a bottle of water, and cough drops—and missing me intensely, of course. And me, going to bed burdened with the guilt of abandonment. Not to worry; absence makes the heart grow fonder. By the end of the week, his cold was much improved, and he was more himself.

One night, after nature had awakened me, I thought I heard voices and noticed a bright light under our bedroom door. If I didn't know my husband better, I would have guessed that he was entertaining. When I cracked the door and peeked in, there was my poor, lonely husband, sprawled across the entire bed laughing hysterically at *The Late Late Show* on TV while noshing on Popchips and sipping Diet Coke. The open newspaper lay on my side of the bed flapping in the wind like a flag mounted atop a pole on a windy day, as the overhead fan whirled furiously, rocking back and forth. A dangling chain swung like a pendulum on steroids, clicking against the light fixture. I closed the door quietly and returned to my bed, unable to forget the scene I had just witnessed—reminding me of a long-ago visit to a friend's college dorm. It had been a long time indeed since our bedroom had hosted that level of activity!

The following morning, I gave John the long-awaited good news that he seemed well enough for me to return to our bed.

And these were his exact words: "Oh, we don't want to rush it, hon. Remember that speech! And that eulogy."

It can happen so fast. One day you're side-by-side in your marriage bed—the next, you've been replaced by a stand-up monologue, a newspaper, some wind, and a bag of Popchips.

The next blow came days later at church, of all places. I love summer because there's no choir, and I get to sit in a pew along-side John—shoulder to shoulder, sharing a hymnal and church bulletin. When it's time to "pass the peace," we always kiss before greeting our friends. I've been told my husband and I are an inspiration to younger couples.

But on this particular morning, as we stood, I opened our hymnal to the next song and was taken aback when my husband reached for his *own* hymnal. When it was time to pass the peace, I stood puckering as John shook my hand. Who'd have dreamed it could happen to us?

At dinner that evening, I was still coming to terms with the shocking events of the week. Afterwards in the kitchen, when we always clean up together, John waved me aside saying, "Go write something; I can do this by myself." (At first, I was horrified, but decided I could live with that one.) It was evening, after all, and almost time for our stroll. It was my favorite part of the day—a period of handholding and sharing.

As we were walking and enjoying a stimulating conversation about our neighbor's psoriasis, and people who don't pick up after their dogs, and the need for speed bumps in the driveway, John suddenly dropped my hand, put on his headset, and charged ahead, listening to the Orioles game.

A cautionary tale, to be sure. Each day of married life is a slippery slope of separation. I shudder to think what's next. Just saying.

→ IT MUST BE MAGIC ←

Michael,

*I*f you're not too busy with your little podcast friends, maybe you'd like to hear about our week.

Your father and I were struck by lightning on Wednesday. It wasn't a direct hit, of course, or we'd be dead, and you'd have heard about it already. It came crashing into our condo about 10:00 a.m. and lit up our kitchen like a supernova. It was followed by a boom louder than that cannon shot at Fort McHenry that left us half-deaf for two days.

At the time, we were having a special breakfast to celebrate the completion of our income taxes. Your father saved ninety dollars by doing them himself, and it only took him 137 hours and nearly cost him his marriage of over half a century. Except for the back of his head, I hadn't seen him since February. I was like a Meals on Wheels volunteer delivering food to a shut-in. Albeit a shut-in with a calculator, a telephone, a computer, and a tablet—who was buried in little pieces of paper and used salty language. I didn't hang around.

I had set the breakfast table, complete with flowers, in the sunroom. Not that there was any sun on Wednesday. It was, in fact, one of those kite-flying kind of days—well, if you're Benjamin Franklin. Rain, wind, thunder, lightning...

"Hey hon, you know what would be good on this English muffin?"

Dad said, pushing away from the table. "Some of those grape preserves."

"No, no, I'll get it," I said, heading for the refrigerator, because between you and me, the muffins would have been moldy by the time your father found the preserves.

I grabbed the refrigerator door handle, and that's when it happened. Honestly, Mike, it was a scene right out of Frankenstein. A blinding flash of light, crashing thunder, three smoke detectors and a fire alarm going off, and somebody screaming (that might have been me).

Anyway, my hand flew from the door handle like it was a hot curling iron, and I spun around to see smoke coming from the back of the television. Your father appeared to be coming back down to the floor—reminding me of a scene from The Flying Nun. In this case, a flying cursing nun.

"What the hell! It's Armageddon!" he yelled, landing on his feet and staring at the smoking television—which smelled worse than a smoldering tea towel on a red-hot burner. (I speak from experience, unfortunately.)

We tried to hug, but that's hard to do while you're holding your ears.

As you know, Mike, Dad and I aren't accustomed to excitement. We lead simple lives. This Tuesday, for example, was a typical day for us. After taking our tax returns to the post office, we went to a viewing, and while they are always sad, they can be uplifting too. Like your father says, "At least that's not one of us in there."

After the viewing, we visited our ninety-five-year-old friend at the nursing home. Jane was playing Bingo, so we joined her. She talked nonstop, played her three cards, kept an eye on our four cards, and won three times. Dad says she should be visiting us.

It's funny how people react in the wake of a calamity. I'm ashamed to say that after we disabled the alarms and called 911, my initial concern was not the possible human toll of the disaster, but rather the fried television in the corner and how long it would take to replace it. For normal people, that would mean going out and making a purchase. Not for your father, though. For him it means consumer guides, exhaustive research, comparison shopping, and a chart with brand names, performance history, and prices. It took him a month to buy light bulbs. The future seemed dim.

Our breathing was still returning to normal when Dad ran down and let the firemen in, and I checked on some neighbors. There was extensive damage, but no injuries, fortunately. Bob said the lightning blew his telephone right off the wall. Ann's fuse box took a direct hit, and she was without electricity. Charles said that two of his TVs blew up.

Dad greeted me at the door with his tablet when I returned.

"Hey Peg, I've been researching lightning strikes, and guess what?! According to this, you and I were in the presence of a super intense electrical charge!"

He followed me through the condo where I turned on ceiling fans and opened the kitchen door to get rid of the lingering odor.

"And listen to this. It's a commonly held belief that lightning is mystical and magical—often leaving victims with freakish super-human powers." His eyes were as round as golf balls.

"Oh, John, you don't believe that nonsense, do you?"

"I believe this article I found in Psychology Today[1]. It says right here that the enormous discharge of electricity from lightning can have a positive effect on the way the brain functions."

We sat on the sofa together, and your father read me a story about a forty-two-year-old New York surgeon. During his recovery from a frightening lightning strike, he started hearing music in his head.

1   Berit Brogaard, D.M.Sci., Ph.D., "Struck by Lightning," *Psychology Today,* April 26, 2013.

"What do you think he did?" asked your father. "He bought a piano and taught himself to play."

I laughed.

Dad pointed to his tablet. "He left his career in medicine and became a classical musician! It's documented!"

"John, we didn't sustain a direct hit," I reminded him.

"But we were surrounded by an enormous electrical charge. You never know!"

And that's when our lives changed.

Since last Wednesday morning, your father has been on the lookout for signs of superhuman, freakish powers. When he left for his daily walk that afternoon, he said, "Don't expect me back anytime soon. I might have a sudden power surge and end up in New Jersey. Don't worry about me." He slid his little flip phone into his pocket and gave it a pat. He was back in one hour, like always—but undiscouraged.

As usual, I played the piano for our church service that evening.

"Maybe you won't get all nervous and make mistakes," Dad said. "Remember, lightning can have a positive effect on the way the brain functions."

My friend Pat congratulated me after the service.

"You sounded good, Peg. I only counted six mistakes, and they were minor."

I'm sure it was meant as a compliment.

When I was leaving for choir rehearsal on Thursday evening, your father gave me a wink, and I knew he hadn't given up hope.

"Maybe you'll be singing a solo on Sunday."

I rolled my eyes. We both know that, though I read music well, my faint voice can barely be heard beyond the choir loft.

On the way to my car, our neighbor Charles pulled in with two brand-new TVs in the back of a pickup. I eyed them with envy.

One look at my expression when I returned from rehearsal, and your father was his old comforting self.

"You're still a valuable choir member, hon. Choral singing is all about voices blending. You know that."

And that's when he made a comment that left me weak in the knees.

"Hey Peg, I think we should replace our fried kitchen TV with one of those newfangled flat screens. What do you say?"

On Friday morning, we walked into Best Buy and bought the first television we saw. No consumer guides, no comparison shopping.

"This one has a good, sharp picture," your father said. "You like this one, Peg? We'll take it."

And now I know, Mike. There really is magic in lightning. Not that I recommend it.

We love you,
Mom

→ PARTY ANIMALS—NOT ←

*J*BLAME IT ON MY OLD FRIENDS. EVERY TIME we get together it's the same thing: a three-hour session of "our-family-is-so-close-can-you-top-this?" marathon.

"Every July our kids spend a week with us at the beach," says Lucy. "Family swims, boisterous meals, and at the end of the day, games and chitchat."

I've always dreamt of a vacation like that.

Mary's children and grandchildren gather at their western Maryland getaway several times a year where they have a dining room table that seats twenty.

How I envy my friends as, one by one, they relive storybook reunions.

When Dora tells us about her family's trek to an idyllic mountain cabin where they spend the evenings reminiscing around the fire, it sounds like a reunion of *The Waltons*. Maybe it's time to plan a family get-together of my own—one where there isn't a long box with a lid in the room or a tasteful urn.

Either that, or I need to get myself some new friends.

I shared my idea about a family gathering with John. "My seventieth birthday is next month. We could have a family reunion birthday party! Whaddaya say?"

John rolled his eyes. "Let's face it. We are not party people. Remember the party when I set the yard on fire?"

Yes, there had been a fire, but it had turned out well. My husband had chosen the day of Mike's birthday party to do his spring burn-off in the field. It wasn't his fault that an unexpected wind came in from the north.

"But the kids loved the fire engines. Remember how nice those firemen were?" I said.

"I remember how the kids were covered in soot and smelled like a bonfire when their parents picked them up," John said. Leave it to my husband to see the dark side.

"But the kids claimed it was the best birthday party they'd been to. Remember?"

"They were five years old, Peg," my Eeyore said. "How many birthday parties had they been to?"

It's true. John and I have never been party people. Our first memorable get-together was a dinner in 1961. By three in the afternoon, there were two fire engines and a fire marshal's car in our front yard, firemen with hoses on the rooftop squirting water down our chimney, and an apartment filled with smoke and wet ashes. We greeted our company looking like we'd spent the day in a charcoal pit.

"Well," I said, "they were *theme* parties."

John rolled his eyes again. "And remember the time we invited the Millers to dinner and forgot to open the vents in our new fireplace?"

We both laughed at this one. "How could I forget? You couldn't see two feet in front of your face because of the smoke, but they were too nice to mention it. They kept saying, 'Everything looks . . . *cough, cough, cough* . . . so pretty! *Cough, cough, cough.*'"

"Would you just settle for burning down the trash corral across the road for your seventieth?" John asked. "The neighbors could gather round and sing 'Happy Birthday.'"

"Very funny," I said. And then my husband really got my attention.

"Do you remember my sixtieth birthday party?"

This time I rolled *my* eyes. "Like I could ever forget that!"

I had explained to our boys (who am I kidding; they were three grown men living on their own) that in lieu of gifts, our friends would be sharing some *lighthearted* remembrances of their father. "So think of a favorite father/son memory to share," I told them.

I could tell by the gleam in their eyes that they were enthusiastic, but when they smirked and raised their eyebrows, I saw a red flag.

"It should be something nice, of course—like the time Dad stayed up all night typing a term paper you put off until the last minute. Or the countless good books you and Dad have shared. That father/son camping trip with the Scouts. Oh, I know. Dad reading from the Bible on Christmas Eve . . ."

"It's okay, Mom. We know what to do," said Scott.

Why would I worry? John was a good father. Sure, he'd had a serious nature when the boys were young, but fatherhood is an awesome responsibility. Of course, there was his frugal streak, but that was understandable for a child of the Depression who had been on his own since his teens. Then there was John's superhuman patience for tedious detail, but that was endearing. Wasn't it?

It was time for the party, and everything was ready—suitcases shoved out of sight, fresh flowers throughout the house, the aromas of lasagna and fresh bread in the air, and John's clothes laid out on the bed. (When your husband is notorious for dressing down, you leave nothing to chance.) So why was I nervous? Maybe it was that unpleasantness earlier in the day when John couldn't find his favorite jeans.

"You've thrown them away!" he accused me in front of our sons, who looked on, amused. They were no strangers to these indignant "You've thrown out my favorite clothes!" confrontations.

"I have not," I said, forcing myself to look him straight in the eye. "They're probably in the laundry."

"I've looked! Just because they have a few imperfections is no reason to give my most comfortable jeans to Goodwill!"

I wanted to tell him that Goodwill was not that desperate but thought better of it. I pictured the tattered jeans I'd hidden on the basement shelf—step one in my discard process. If all went well, they'd be in the trash on Monday morning. The boys knew the drill. There was a time when they'd been accomplices in burying their father's rags.

How many times on trash night had I handed the boys an article of clothing that had been hidden for days or even weeks, and whispered, "Quick! You know what to do. Push it as far down in the can as you can. Out of sight!" Oh yeah, our boys were savvy.

John's birthday party was progressing beautifully. My parents were there, and John's two Maryland brothers and a sister-in-law, as well as several of our closest friends. Most importantly, our three sons were all together, along with Scott's wife, Marjie, and our two young, perfect granddaughters—about twenty-five of us in all.

After dinner, we took turns sharing sweet, funny stories that brought bursts of laughter. Two friends gave John a lovely sweater (so much for no gifts), saying, "We're tired of you being such a dull dresser!" I wanted to say, "Now see here, my husband has lovely clothes hanging in the closet he has never worn. It's not my fault he chooses to dress like a bum!"

Considering there was neither smoke nor fire that evening, there was a lot of roasting going on.

An old college buddy presented my husband with an enlarged photograph of himself and a much younger John taken after another, shall we say, "rousing" party. Our sons loved the out-of-character picture of their father—fully clothed, bleary eyed, and sitting in an empty bathtub with his friend, Norman, talking into the wee hours of the morning. What the photo didn't show was me standing impatiently in the bathroom doorway, car keys jangling in my hand.

When it came time for the children's tribute, our youngest son handed his father a plain white box. Printed on top in large black letters was RAGS 'R' US.

John smiled like a kid on Christmas morning as he lifted the infamous tattered jeans from the box. They were little more than a zipper, belt loops, and a series of holes held together by a few denim threads. The room rocked with laughter. Then his sons began their tribute.

"First of all, let me say that I have never seen this house so bright. We had very dim bulbs when we were growing up which we were not allowed to turn on. Teachers were bewildered by the wax drippings on my homework."

My jaw dropped. "He's exaggerating!" I cried out, but I couldn't be heard over the laughter, none louder than John's.

"I was teaching you economy, son."

"He turned off the heat at night!" Mike told his audience. "The hairs in my nose were iced up in the morning, and the upstairs toilet couldn't be flushed until the spring thaw!"

"Yeah," said Scott. "You told me I was lazy when I threw my clothes on the bed instead of hanging them up. I was avoiding frostbite!"

"Hey, I put in a woodstove!" countered John.

"You turned me into a frontiersman," said Scott. "While my friends were at the mall eating burgers and fries, I was sawing down trees and splitting firewood."

"I taught you survival!" John was getting into the spirit.

"Survival?" said Phil. "I got up every morning and shoveled ashes; kids at school thought I was prematurely gray! I was too busy stacking logs and feeding a woodstove to do my homework."

"Remember when the woodstove was new?" Mike recalled to his brothers. "For weeks, Dad walked from room to room holding up a giant thermometer in one hand and carrying a notebook in the other, looking like the poor man's Statue of Liberty."

Scott mimicked his father's deep voice. "Do you believe this? It's ten degrees colder upstairs than in the kitchen, and five degrees warmer in this closet. And look what happens when I hold the thermometer near the ceiling."

Mike picked up the pace. "Just look at this graph, boys. December 3rd at 10:00 *a.m.*—69 degrees in the living room; December 3rd, 10:00 *p.m.*—79 degrees in the living room. This is fascinating stuff."

"Yeah," said Phil. "Fascinating that I was a seventh grader who had singed eyebrows and smelled like a bonfire. Teachers kept ordering me to hand over my cigarettes."

———

When the party ended, I decided that family get-togethers in real life can be unpredictable, so I decided on something quieter for my seventieth. John picked up a pizza, and we watched a couple of reruns of *The Waltons*.

We did light a bunch of candles around the room—just for old times' sake.

RED, WHITE, AND BROWN:
→ THE PRICE OF CELEBRITY ←

*L*ONG BEFORE SOCIAL MEDIA AND REALITY TV made it possible for everybody and his brother to be a celebrity, I was a confident fifteen-year-old experiencing my very own fifteen minutes of fame—though "infamy" would be a more appropriate description.

It was 1953, and the Overlea Lions Club, along with other local service organizations—possibly the Kiwanis or Rotary Club—was organizing a Fourth of July parade. I knew this because my father, a longtime Lion, was on the parade committee.

"Hon, do you think you and your friends would like to ride your horses in the Fourth of July parade?" he asked me one day. "We have community groups marching and dignitaries riding in open convertibles, but it would sure liven things up to have some prancing horses. What do you think?"

Anyone who has ever been to a parade knows the exhilaration triggered by prancing horses. More than once I had imagined myself astride one of these magnificent creatures.

Now I pictured myself on my prancing gray horse with crowds of people lining the road, cheering. So, giving little thought to the fact that Jet was young and green, I made, quite possibly, the most ill-advised decision of my young life.

"Gee, Dad, that sounds like fun! Let me ask my friends." I closed my eyes briefly. "I can name six people right off the bat, and they have friends. . . ."

What was I thinking? Jet's world was a quiet pasture with thick shade trees and a flowing stream. His daily excitement came when Henny Penny clucked softly and laid an egg in the corner of his stall.

My friends thought a parade sounded like a super idea, and on the morning of the Fourth, our horse brigade clip-clopped along the hard-surfaced side streets leading to Belair Road. There were twelve of us in all. It was like being part of a cavalry regiment, and I had never felt more important.

There was excitement in the air, as well as the odor of fly repellant we had sprayed on our horses. A sight to behold, we were a spirited display of Independence Day patriotism—making our way up Kenwood Avenue toward our ill-fated destiny.

Harold, wearing an American flag shirt, led the way on his big white mare, Lady. He was a year or so older than I was, and all the girls had a crush on him—or maybe I just imagined it. Spirit personified, Lady was the kind of horse that strained at the bit and liked to be first. Harold's sister, a high school cheerleader, had supplied the red and blue pom-poms for Lady's mane and forelock that gave her the appearance of a circus horse.

My friend Judy, aboard her bay gelding, was in red pants and a blue-and-white striped blouse. Beneath her horse's saddle was a bright red blanket.

Mom had knitted my blue-and-white striped saddle blanket and found some matching ribbons for Jet's mane and tail. I was wearing enough fringe to outfit the NYC Rockettes. The other horses and riders were likewise adorned, and together, we were about to "liven up" the first Overlea Fourth of July parade—beyond my father's wildest expectations.

Someone had made a banner that said, *The Power Line Pleasure Riders*. I had come up with the name, as our favorite trails followed the electric power lines through the local countryside. Riders on the two quietest horses volunteered to carry the banner. They would go first, with Lady, straining at the bit, close behind.

I positioned myself between two of the calmer, more mature animals. None of the horses or riders had ever been in a parade before.

For obvious reasons, our position was pretty much at the end of the parade—behind the marching band, which was complete with baton twirlers and an array of brass horns. The drums were at the rear, along with a glockenspiel and cymbals.

What could possibly go wrong?

Behind us, were two engines from the local volunteer fire department, as well as police cars and an ambulance—all of which were a reassuring presence.

Fortunately, some of the details of the parade itself are somewhat blurred. Experts tell us that our brains block unpleasant experiences to protect us from recurring nightmares.

Things began calmly enough, with innocent families lining the curb—standing and seated in folding chairs, strollers, and wheelchairs—waving American flags. There was yelling and applauding, just as I had imagined. Some were even taking our pictures, and I knew then how it felt to be a celebrity.

Actually, it was the last thing I clearly remember before the brass horns in the marching band gave their opening salvo—a Sousa fanfare that could be heard in Minneapolis. We were opposite the Overlea Diner when it happened.

Jet flew a couple of feet off the ground, like one of those bottle rockets that take off so fast you lose sight of them. Seconds later, he landed hard, stiff legged, his head thrown so high his mane slapped my face. With his tail raised, his entire body vibrated like my mother's washing machine when the towels were clumped together on one side. Then he pretty much exploded. He wasn't the only one.

Everywhere, panicking horses showing the whites of their eyes—rearing, bucking, and snorting—as though a whirling spaceship had landed in our midst. Riders were flying into the air as innocent bystanders grabbed kids and backed away from the street so fast, they lost their balance and fell over.

And the band played on, oblivious to the chaos directly behind them—until Lady charged ahead, prancing into the marching music makers, her pom-poms erect and high above the instruments. Other horses spun around and headed for the hills, only to come face-to-face with sirens, flashing lights, and blaring horns. Through it all, the spinning horses were like fire hoses spewing manure—manure of the loose variety. It splattered on fire trucks, on the streets, on drums and cymbals, and on traumatized marchers.

At one point, Jet slipped and came to an abrupt halt, as he was temporarily blinded by the banner that had blown over his face. I'm pretty sure I was thrown to the street and landed on my feet, only to quickly remount before I could be trampled. As I've said, specifics are blurry.

The good news is that no one died on that Fourth of July— including the marching band members and the spectators who had run for their lives. Apparently, an ambulance driver gave first aid to two tuba players after they'd been stepped on by an enormous white horse with pom-poms. Word was that they were more upset by the manure on their instruments than their superficial injuries.

The Power Line Pleasure Riders didn't finish the parade that day. After the unseated riders were reunited with their mounts, we headed back down Kenwood Avenue like a cavalry regiment after a grueling battle.

By the time we reached the little grocery store on Dale Avenue, we could no longer hear the sirens and music, and the horses were plodding along like work animals—except for Lady, of course, who only had one speed, and whose lovely white tail and legs were as brown as the manure piled alongside my barn.

We treated ourselves to a soda and a Tastykake. It was a while before we could laugh about it.

The biggest takeaway from the day occurred later that night. I was leaving the bathroom when I heard laughter behind my parents' closed bedroom door. Then the voice of my father—a mild-mannered man who never used foul language. Perhaps that's why, sixty-six years later, I can recall his exact words:

"I guarantee you, hon, those firemen will be scrubbing horse shit off of that engine for days to come." Laughter. "And who knows how long it will take to get it out of the streetcar tracks." Laughter. "And those poor kids in the marching band . . ." Laughter. "Go to war Miss Agnes!"

They were still laughing when I turned out my light.

———◆•◆———

It was the first—and last—Fourth of July parade in Overlea that I can remember. As parades go, it was pretty darn lively.

Ahh, the price of celebrity.

Happy 4th of July, Mike! Went to Towson parade this morning—and cried! Just like my grandma. Everything makes me cry these days: little girls twirling batons, soldiers marching in formation, the flag... It's embarrassing! Tonight is the Baltimore Symphony's annual patriotic concert under the stars. We'll be there with lawn chairs, insect repellent—and a box of tissues.

Fortunately, it will be dark.

⤙ THE RAPTURE ⤚

Hi Mike,

*D*ad and I just came in from a church dinner. These get-togethers always remind me of the Wednesday night Lenten
dinners we used to have during Easter season when you boys were
growing up. Not much has changed—except that our congregation
is smaller these days, and grayer.

You met your first girlfriend at church, remember? It meant we
no longer had to force you out the door on Sunday mornings. That
was nice. I've decided to share a somewhat similar experience I had
at a slightly younger age than you. I don't think I've ever told you
about it. I hope it won't be too embarrassing.

I was thirteen. I remember this because it was the year Johnnie
Ray recorded the song "Cry," and women, including my teenaged
friends and older sister, couldn't get enough of the famous celebrity.
Nana and Pop took my sister and me to the Steel Pier in Atlantic City
to a live concert featuring the heartthrob. Your Aunt Janet was all
agog. What an eye-opener! Screaming young women took off their
underwear and threw it onto the stage. There was practically a riot.

This was also the year our church hired a new music director
and the year my hormones kicked in (TMI, I know—sorry). James
was our church's first male music director. Once, when my mother—
your nana—was talking on the telephone to her sister about Gregory

Peck, I overheard her use the expression "Bigger than life and twice as handsome." I thought it was a perfect description for James, who towered above everyone in the choir. I'm telling you, Mike, Johnnie Ray couldn't hold a hymnal to this Adonis. Whether he was speaking or singing, his powerful, deep voice reverberated through my body like an exploding Fourth of July firecracker.

Those women and girls in the choir loft weren't fooling me for one second. It wasn't a passion for music that brought them out to Thursday rehearsals and the Sunday morning services. Oh no. Their eyes bored into their leader's face like a woodburning tool, and I'm willing to bet that more than one of them had impure thoughts.

My parents were delighted that I had at last seen the light and accompanied them to church willingly. No longer having to be hunted down on Sunday mornings and threatened with the loss of privileges, I was now the first one in the car. The daughter who didn't want to be seen with her mother and father now sat beside them willingly during the Sunday services. My change in attitude was nothing less than miraculous, and they thanked the almighty Lord.

Silly parents.

Those of you who are "unchurched" (that's the modern-day vernacular for people who sleep in on Sunday mornings) are probably unaware that regular churchgoers—Presbyterians in particular—are like Ravens and Orioles season ticket holders. You always know where they'll be sitting during a home game (or in this case, during church service on Sunday mornings). They never deviate, and God forbid some innocent visitor should be in their seat when they arrive for service.

My parents sat midway on the center aisle—pulpit side—always surrounded by the same people. Every Sunday morning was like a family reunion until, of course, the organ prelude began. Then it was as solemn as a funeral service. Of course, Mom and Dad were more than delighted to have their thirteen-year-old daughter join them. Ordinarily, I would sit way at the back of the church or in the balcony with friends, where we discussed everything but religion—and where it was all the easier to sneak out during interminable sermons, then back in during the last hymn.

Now, my mother gave a little sniff and held her head high as if to say to those around us, "See? We did raise our daughter right!" It was no coincidence that I sat on the end of the pew. Even on those Sundays I had to stand up and step into the aisle so that Dad could slip out and help with the morning offering or communion. I insisted on sitting on the end. I had convinced my parents that I had a touch of claustrophobia. But, of course, my motive was much more devious.

At the beginning of each service, the choir processed from the back of the church, with James following close behind, guarding their flanks, like a conscientious Border Collie shepherding his flock down the aisle to the choir loft at the front of the church. His powerful voice vibrated the stained glass windows the way the front end of our old lawn tractor vibrated the driver.

And here's where the strategy came into play. I waited for the choristers to pass by, walking two by two like the animals boarding the Ark—then quickly edged into the aisle. Timing and position were crucial, but if I got it just right, James would brush against my arm or shoulder as he passed, turning my entire body into your grandmother's homemade grape jelly and making me weak in the knees—kind of like that Christmas I sneaked into the dining room and drained the wine decanter.

At the end of the service, the choir recessed, and I got to stare at the face of this Greek god with that serious, no nonsense demeanor. The rapture stayed with me for the entire week. More than once I had felt betrayed by a God who had not bestowed upon me an angelic voice, worthy of a front row seat in the choir loft.

The turning point came a couple of years later, and believe you me, that's a long time to be in a state of euphoria. It happened on the

Easter Sunday morning James brought his wife and five children to visit the church where he worked. Who knew? It just wasn't the same after that. Not that he wasn't still fun to stare at and listen to, but that was the year I fell head over heels in love with a big gray horse—and life went on.

As I've said, Mike, I hope my confession wasn't too shocking. And in my defense, I never once removed my underwear and threw it at my beloved. Historians will probably look back at this incident and chalk it up to one teenager's celebrity crush. For me, it was just a small part of the magic of growing up in Kenwood Church. I'm sure you have similar memories, but I don't need to hear them.

Love you,
Mom

⇢ MOTHER LOVE ⇠

*M*Y BOOK, *ABOUT MY MOTHER*, CONTINUES to do well. People can't get enough of my mom. Of course, I didn't tell *everything* in my book—I held some things back. I wanted my mother to be a sympathetic character, after all. One story, especially, didn't make the cut. I'm sharing it now because I've thought of a way to justify my mother's shocking behavior. I can chalk it up to "mother love."

It was 1946 when the Paramount Theater opened. The Paramount wasn't just any theater. It was the largest, most modern movie house for miles around, showing first-run features like *Gone with the Wind* and *The Wizard of Oz*.

Our community was fortunate, for sure, as through the years, the Paramount stage was the go-to venue for such avant-garde activities as a world-class yoyo presentation and tournament, a Saturday morning hula hoop demonstration and competition, and a rope jumping gala. It was impossible to see a kid on the sidewalks of our town who didn't have either a yoyo, a hula hoop, or a jump rope that year.

In 1949, the Paramount sponsored the first ever Miss Overlea Beauty Pageant—an activity that would reveal a side of my mother that shocked me to the core.

Pictures of five pretty, wholesome, local teens were displayed in the lobby, kind of like pictures of sandwiches are displayed at Subway shops today. They were neighborhood celebrities, to be sure.

Moviegoers were encouraged to vote for their favorite "girl next door" by writing her name on a piece of paper and dropping it in the ballot box. The winner would be crowned Miss Overlea, and the five runners-up would be members of her court, or ladies in waiting.

And here's the weird part. Somehow my dignified fifteen-year-old sister was one of the contestants. Now, I knew my modest older sister very well, and there was no way she would have initiated this. She was not the type! Even if she was pretty and excelled at everything she tried, she was not a show-off.

More than one of Janet's former schoolteachers had seen my name on their roster for the coming year and thanked the gods for their good fortune in having another one of the Knobel girls in their class. Naturally, I cleared up any of those illusions in the first week of school.

I might have resented my achieving older sister, had it not been for her sweet disposition. Janet reached the very pinnacle of "coolness" the day we were seated in the back seat of cousin Jimmy's convertible while he was showing off behind the wheel. She turned and whispered something in my ear that was so uncharacteristic, it took my breath away.

"He thinks he's hot shit!" she said. Well, it was like one of those religious movies where Jesus performs a miracle, and choirs of angels sing in the background. Janet had shown her mortal side, and I loved her for it, as cousin Jimmy was far from my favorite person.

⎯⎯⧱◆⧲⎯⎯

It's hard to believe, but for some reason, my mother was proud that her daughter's picture was hanging in a movie theater lobby, like criminals hang on a post office wall. As anyone who knew her will attest, my mother had a slightly competitive nature. Slightly as in "the habanero pepper is *slightly* hot." And this was a chance to have our own family celebrity. Imagine being the mother of Miss Overlea. It is said that parents like to live vicariously through their children. Perhaps it had been my mother's dream to be a beauty queen and a celebrity herself.

One day after school, Mom handed me my jacket, the roomy one with the big pockets, and said she needed my help. I assumed it was window washing or garden weeding day, but instead, she led the way to the car and drove us up to Belair Road where she parked in front of Woolworth's, just across the street from the Paramount Theater. She reached for her purse.

This was puzzling, as we were not a family of moviegoers. In fact, we hardly ever went because when it came to movies, my mother set a high bar. I heard my father tell her once, "You should be on that censor board, hon." She was in charge of molding her daughters' character, after all—a job she took very seriously.

"Are we going to the movies on a Thursday afternoon?" I asked. The marquee showed a double feature: *Son of Frankenstein* and *Blood of the Beasts*. My sister and I weren't even allowed to see *The Three Stooges*. Before I could say anything else, my mother turned to me.

"Peggy," she said with all seriousness, like she was getting ready to lead the Women of the Church in prayer. "You know that those other girls on the wall"—she nodded her head toward the theater—"can't hold a candle to your sister, right? Not only is she prettier, she's smart, and respectable." More than once I'd heard my mother say that my sister had enough poise and grace for the entire neighborhood. And it was true.

"Janet deserves to win that contest. Don't you agree?"

And then it occurred to me what was happening. My mother was taking me, the family goof-off and troublemaker, into her confidence, as though I were a trusted friend and not an eleven-year-old who regularly embarrassed her. Heady stuff, indeed, so why did I have the feeling I was going to be an accomplice in a crime? What if she asked me to go into the lobby of the Paramount Theater and splash paint on the pictures of the other girls? Would I do it? I pictured my own photograph hanging on the post office wall.

Now I was being silly. My mother would be the last person on earth to do something unlawful. She was a person of great integrity, this woman who wouldn't even allow her daughters to engage in gossip. "If you can't say something nice, don't say anything at all!" was one of her favorite admonishments. This was a woman who had made me turn around and walk back to the store because I had only been charged for one candy bar when I had bought two.

This paragon of propriety and virtue pulled dozens of slips of paper from her purse—some white, some yellow, some lined, and some plain—and she handed half of them to me, along with a pen, some colored pencils, and a black marker. I might not have known a lot of big words in those days, but I did know one: *premeditation*. And this was it.

"All you have to do is write Janet's name on those papers and fold them. Some of those girls come from big families that go to the movies all the time. We hardly ever go to the movies, so the voting isn't really fair, is it?"

My mother, president of the Women of the Church, and I were sitting on the front seat of our Chevy wagon like Ma Barker and her kid casing the bank before a heist. I laid my papers on the open door of the glove compartment and did as I was told—switching pencils, writing neatly, then slanting my words backwards like my friend Rosy, then printing. I thought back to the day I had signed my mother's name on a failing test paper. You'd have thought I had burned down an orphanage on Christmas day when she found out. And here I was spelling Knobel wrong on purpose. A lot of people made that mistake. They were always reversing the "l" and the "e" or leaving off the "K." Ma Barker used her leather purse for a desk, writing in ink, then in pencil, left-handed, then right-handed, until all the slips of paper were folded.

My eyes were as round as the horn in the middle of our old Chevy's steering wheel, and I stopped breathing when a man came from Woolworth's five-and-dime store a few yards away and headed straight for our car. I slid way down in my seat and covered my face. Fortunately, he walked right on by.

Mom tapped her watch and looked across the street. "The two o'clock matinee lets out in three minutes," she said. "You can act like you just saw the movie, and you're coming out with the rest." *Premeditation* . . . She looked at me over her glasses. "You know, the way you used to sneak out of church, then blend in with people leaving after the service." (And I thought I was so clever.) "When nobody's looking, slip these into the ballot box. Here, put them in your pocket." Her head was held high, as though she were performing some lofty community service.

I learned something about myself that day. I'm not good with intrigue. I broke out in a cold sweat as I walked into that lobby with a pocketful of paper slips that felt like little sticks of dynamite. On the other hand, my mother had entrusted me with a sensitive mission, and this was my chance to get in her good graces.

People exited through the inner doors, and several lined up at the ballot box. I got at the end of the line. When a girl got behind me, I stepped out of line to look at the pictures lining the lobby walls—Elizabeth Taylor, Clark Gable, Judy Garland . . .

When the last person in line left and the ticket taker disappeared through the inner doors, I hurried to the ballot box and stuffed the papers through the slot. Mission accomplished! Then, full of self-importance, I headed out the door and noticed that my getaway car had made a U-turn on Belair Road and was idling in front of the theater. In a clever bit of strategy, Ma Barker had turned the horses for home! I climbed in, and she drove to Kenwood Avenue where we turned left—in total silence.

Well, Audrey Schultz was crowned Miss Overlea that year. She was one of seven children, all of whom undoubtedly went to the movies seven days a week and stuffed the ballot box every single time. Some people! I was secretly glad my sister didn't win, though I never said as much to my mother. I have a feeling she was relieved also. Knowing that her daughter had won dishonestly would probably have kept Mom up nights. And really, celebrity is overrated.

The incident was never mentioned again.

Mother love is a funny thing.

⇥ HAPPY BIRTHDAY, FIRSTBORN ⇤

Hi Mike,

I've always been a positive, upbeat person—you know that. But when my oldest son turns fifty-seven and he's 9,000 miles away in Sydney, Australia, it's hard to smile.

So how do I acknowledge such a momentous occasion without indulging in that sappy, Hallmark sentimentality you detest? I'm not going to eulogize your fifty-seven years as a perfect son who has made us proud every day and continues to bring us joy—because that would embarrass you. Nor will I describe the terror I felt when I first laid eyes on my helpless baby boy, completely dependent on Dad and me—because that would be way too earnest. And I certainly don't want to describe the feeling of peace and well-being that washed over me as I nursed my blue-eyed bundle—or the sentiment that, at such times, you and I were the only two people in the world. Nah! That would be far too sentimental!

So, instead of cooking your favorite meal and giving you a book by your favorite author, I pulled out the photo albums. I was trying to figure out how long it has been since your father and I had the privilege of celebrating your birthday where you were actually in the room.

I still don't know because, as usual, I got sidetracked—this time with pictures from Scott and Marjie's wedding twenty-seven years ago—and a paper napkin with some scribbling. You gave the toast at your brother's reception, remember? But since there were no cell phones and no videographer, you probably don't recall what you said. Fortunately, I do—with the help of a paper napkin.

As usual, you were very entertaining—even if you weren't totally accurate. You spoke of the dubious honor of being the first-born son.

"At one time in history," you observed, "such a position would have guaranteed me a privileged status and the inheritance of our father's estate." At this point, you looked over at Dad and smiled.

"Being the firstborn son in our family," you lamented, "guaranteed me a guinea pig status and the inheritance of two obsessive, rookie parents."

I laughed and looked up from the napkin where I was scribbling notes—hoping no one would notice.

It was a humorous, lighthearted toast—filled with shameful hyperbole. Guests loved it, and I wondered if you might have a shot as a stand-up comic. At one point, you looked over at me and recalled learning to ride your first bicycle—at the age of six. You described my anxious face peering through the living room window as you pedaled back and forth, back and forth, in the safe confines of our driveway (the part about being on a leash was totally bogus, of course!). Then you told the gathering about your two brothers and their bicycles. "When my younger brothers reached the same age, I watched them pedal their bikes out of sight with a road map, a compass, and a knapsack!" (That part could have been true. Our rules had been somewhat relaxed by that time.)

Who knew you could still recall your first invitation to a boy/girl party in high school, or that your paranoid mother had visited the girl's house beforehand and interviewed her parents? (In the interest of accuracy, it wasn't a real interview. I didn't take notes.) Later, you would calmly mention how your younger brothers casually dropped in at friends' parties in high school—unbeknownst to Dad and me.

You were on a roll with your toast, Mike. You even had vivid memories of learning to drive, while I hyperventilated into a paper bag and screamed from the passenger seat of our old station wagon. When you paused in your toast and looked over at me and said, "I didn't know you could cuss like that, Mom," I had to shake my head no. Then you told how I had taken my knitting along when accompanying Scott while he was learning to drive. (I doubt that very much.)

I was grateful you couldn't remember the doting new mother who changed your outfit every other hour, or the "nervous Nelly" who scrubbed the floor every other day when you learned to crawl. Fortunately, you didn't mention "mellow mother" several years later who picked your baby brother's sippy cup off the floor, blew away the dog hair, and stuck it back in his mouth.

At this point in your toast, Mike, you turned to the bride and groom. "And now, Scott, you and your lovely Marjie are getting married. I wish you all the best for many years to come. You're doing something I have never done. I'm afraid you're on your own, little brother. Good luck! I'll be interested to hear what Mom has planned for your honeymoon."

I laughed along with the others and lifted my glass, grateful that you didn't include the really humiliating stuff.

Of course, you won't be inheriting our entire estate, Mike. But as the firstborn, you will have the privilege of caring for your father and me in our dotage. It's the least we can do for you.

Happy fifty-seventh birthday!

Love,
Mom and Dad

→ ABOUT FACE ←

I OPENED THE DOOR AND STEPPED INTO what looked like an opium den. I've never been in an opium den, of course, but I do watch PBS. And thanks to an Agatha Christie episode of *Hercule Poirot*, it's as if I were there. If it hadn't been for the two lovely girls who greeted me, I'd have turned around and run. At least I think they were two lovely girls. It was difficult to tell in the dim, dusky light.

Had I been blindfolded I'd have thought I was in a candle or potpourri shop. The sweet, pungent fragrance was almost sickening. The background noise, which couldn't really be described as music, was tuneless—devoid of melody and rhythm—with the occasional sound of chirping birds and trickling water.

I thought back to the conversation I'd just had with my husband.

John: "You're getting a what?"

Me, raising my voice: "A *facial,* John—with an *aesthetician.* At a spa. Lots of people get them. I have some trouble areas, and I want to look my best for that big TV interview next week."

John: "You don't need any *facial!*"

You'd have thought I'd made an appointment for a nose job. My husband leaned closer and squinted his eyes. "You look fine to me. And what does an electrician know about a facial?"

I'm not a sophisticated person. My world is not one of mani-
cures and pedicures and massages. Waxing and facials are proce-
dures I've only read about. I don't even have my nails and hair
done—just the occasional haircut.

Yet, here I was at the age of eighty-one, now lying on a bed
in a dimly lit room, covered with a sheet—and wishing I had
listened to my husband.

Oh, well. At least it wasn't a colonoscopy.

There was a dreamlike quality to the lady's voice, though it
was a little creepy when she referred to me as a "facial virgin." Her
voice reminded me of the woman who taught yoga at the gym.
The one who had admonished John and me to save our conversations for the parking lot.

All in all, the steam, the mask, the cool creams, the aroma
of oranges, the hot towels, and the shoulder massages were quite
lovely. This "facial virgin" closed her eyes and dreamt of awak-
ening to flawless, wrinkle-free skin—devoid of age spots—similar
to that of the lovely aesthetician behind my head.

Of course, that didn't happen. But I did hear some funny
stories about men who came for massages with "unrealistic
expectations." And others who had such poor hygiene, they were
refused service.

Would I do it again? Maybe. I did learn a few things. While
there was some improvement, wrinkles and age spots are mine for
life—which John was kind enough to point out.

Next time, I'll definitely avoid drinking water beforehand. An
hour and a half is a long time.

The next day, I would learn how close I had come to having a
real story to tell. At the same time I was having my first ever spa
experience, a police raid and bust was in progress just down the
road at a different massage parlor and day spa. There were multiple
arrests, including at least one high-profile client, with an ongoing
investigation concerning a prostitution and sex trafficking ring.

It was the main topic of conversation during Mahjongg at the community center that week.

And to think I could have gone to that other spa and been falsely arrested for prostitution—and given a lot of people a good laugh.

→ ON BEING A MOTHER ←

J RECENTLY READ A STORY IN *THE NEW YORK Times* about obsessive parents who are too involved in their children's lives. They're called "helicopter parents" and "snowplow parents." They hover and remove obstacles to clear the path for their offspring's success.

Thank heavens I was never one of those! I was just a normal, responsible mother, involved in my children's lives and supportive at every turn. It's what we mothers do: we sign on as room mother, Cub Scout den leader, Sunday School teacher, and the like. I took our sons to Little League and swimming lessons, had their teeth straightened, hernias repaired, lazy eyes corrected, and tonsils removed. I attended plays, choral presentations, and PTA meetings. And I'm here to tell you, it's impossible to quit that kind of support cold turkey, simply because our children become adults!

I was proud as punch and bragged to everybody I knew (as well as some strangers) when Scott earned his Professional Engineer rating. We even had a name plaque made for his desk, but beyond that, have not been involved in his career. Well, we might have visited him in the field . . . and at his office . . . and in the lab. But we were certainly not obtrusive.

When Phil ran a local theater, John and I traveled across three states to attend various plays. When he ran a secondhand bookstore, we regularly visited and left with armloads of precious used books. We might have even given some advice about organizing, but we were not obtrusive.

When our oldest son announced that he was pursuing a career in show business, it was like plowing fresh ground. Nobody in my family had ever been in a business fraught with such potential for failure. Knowing that the odds were against him was incentive to support our son in any way I could. Please keep that in mind as you read my story.

I'm sure any normal mother would have done what I did.

———◆———

Back in June of 1990, I woke up every morning at 3:00 a.m. to watch my son impersonate a salesman on the QVC channel. Naturally, I wanted him to be successful. So, like any good mother and teacher, I didn't just watch—I studied his performance and took copious notes. Then I made a list of helpful tips that would hopefully delay my son's inevitable termination from his first real job in television. I still have carbon copies of those critiques, hand-written in very careful cursive on yellow legal paper.

- Try not to yawn while you're on camera.
- If you're going to yawn on camera, try not to stretch too.
- Don't juggle the Hummels.
- No one wants to know which collectable doll you're attracted to, or why.

Like a stage director, I was giving sage advice. My husband had been doing amateur local theater for years and valued such critiques. But my son apparently wasn't in the mood for advice back then. He would share with me later that his main goal in those early days was just staying awake. I wasn't to be deterred, and I continued sending helpful advice. After all, his career was at stake. And God knows, the boy needed guidance.

- When you talk to viewers on the phone, don't ask them what they're wearing. It's a little creepy.
- Don't describe the products you're selling as "items formerly handed out as prizes on a carnival midway" (even if it is entertaining).
- Don't ask callers what kind of trailer they have until you're certain they live in one.

I despaired when Mike was suspended for "inappropriate contact with a porcelain nun doll" and assigned to the graveyard shift permanently. I tried to give him encouragement.

"Honestly, Michael," I wrote, "you have such potential. If only you'd stop making fun of the products—and the customers. There's no telling how far you could go!"

When it became clear that my son's career in home shopping might never eclipse the graveyard shift, we bought a VCR, and I began taping his shows. This allowed me to evaluate Mike's nocturnal meanderings at a more humane hour and provided him with even more detailed feedback—which is precisely what I did for the next three years.

———⋘◈⋙———

Long after Mike's QVC bosses gave up, I was still trying to inspire him with daily doses of encouragement and practical wisdom.

- Don't describe the yellow topaz pendant as "sputum colored."
- Don't use the jewelry ruler to measure the length of your fingers or the size of the model's ears.

- Do you really suppose the manufacturers of the 10-Piece Unbreakable Outdoor Dinner Service imagined their plates would be cracked over the knee of a host who thought the "unbreakable" nature of their product needed to be tested on live television?

I look back on those QVC days with a mixture of pride—that my son was loved by millions of viewers—and embarrassment—that I might have inadvertently stepped over the line a teensy-weensy bit as an overzealous mother. And so, I'm going to come clean. I hope you'll still respect me afterwards.

A few weeks after Mike was suspended again—this time for an incident involving the existence of Santa Claus—I was desperate. My beloved smart aleck was sabotaging his own career night after night. So, I sat down with my pen and yellow legal pad and, in my very best cursive, wrote a letter to Mike's boss, encouraging him to move my son into a primetime slot.

Naturally, Mike's mother couldn't write such a letter. How would that look? So "Clair Weaver" did the deed. She might have gilded the lily just a tad, but she had a way with words for sure.

"Mike Rowe is the only host who feels like a real person," she wrote. "Why is he hidden away in the middle of the night?" Clair had a good point.

A week later, I followed up with a missive from "Fran Miller" who asked, "Why can't all of your hosts be more like Mike Rowe? He's just so charming and authentic!"

When my first two letters failed to produce the desired result, "JoAnn Adams" offered this: "Your primetime hosts could learn a thing or two from the guy at 3:00 a.m.! That fella is terrific!" Really—somebody had to enlighten the powers that be at QVC.

However futile, it was a great exercise in creativity. I had even talked my husband into driving to nearby towns so that the letters came from different postmarks.

The day Mike presented me with those three letters was one of the most embarrassing moments of my motherhood.

"Here, Mom. My boss read them aloud at weekly staff meetings in a segment he dubbed, 'Letters from Mike Rowe's Mother.' You're a celebrity at QVC."

If there's a bright spot in this story, it is that my son claims I taught him a lot about the unconditional and sometimes desperate support that only a mother can offer.

He's a nice boy.

→ ELEVATOR MAN ←

Hi Mike,

When I came in from shopping, your father said he had just gotten off the phone with you—after half an hour! Most unusual! Funny thing about Dad. As much as he loves to chat with people in person, he can't wait to hand me the telephone. Unless, of course, it's technical support or a telemarketer.

I thought I'd share something about him that most people don't know. Unless they've ever ridden in an elevator with him. In which case, they already know everything about him. I call my little story Elevator Man.

———◆———

I approached the elevator nervously, as I always do, and breathed a sigh of relief when I saw it was unoccupied. I quickly pushed the button for level four, but before the doors could close, several other people appeared from nowhere and joined Dad and me. Among them was a sober, heavyset man with red suspenders and a full white beard. Your father's eyes immediately began to sparkle. I groaned, but, of course, it was too late.

"Hey there, big fella, where did you park your reindeer this morning?"

Your father has always enjoyed familiarity and unsolicited small talk, but it never became a problem until he came across an article in the doctor's waiting room called "The Psychology of Elevator Behavior."

"This is so true!" he said, nodding his head and tapping the magazine with his finger. "People on elevators do clam up and avoid eye contact. I see it all the time." And then Dad looked off into space and wondered, "Now why is that?"

Well, ever since, your father has become a vertical cruise director, determined to replace the awkward silence that defines most elevator rides with the conviviality of a high school reunion. Undaunted by the awkward silence after his question to the heavyset man with the red suspenders and white beard, your father repeated himself, a little louder this time and with a conspiratorial wink.

"I say, so where did you park your reindeer this morning?"

The heavyset man smiled and indulged his inquisitor.

"Oh, I only use the reindeer on Christmas Eve. Their visas expire after twenty-four hours, you know."

Sure enough, the little group looked up from the floor and came to life. When a woman said she heard there was going to be snow for Christmas, Dad beamed the way he did that time a twenty-dollar bill blew across the road in front of us. Mission accomplished!

In early February your father issued a public service announcement to a silent gathering in an elevator in a professional building.

"Don't put your winter coats away," he warned half a dozen strangers. "Punxsutawney Phil saw his shadow this morning." The woman next to him jumped about six inches, then replied, guardedly, "Yes, I just saw that groundhog on the Today show!" Then a conversation ensued. An awkward conversation, but a conversation, nevertheless. It takes so little to make your father happy.

Sadly, not everyone is willing to engage with Chatty Cathy while locked in a metal box, despite his best efforts. More often than not, they stand silently, like the chorus in a Greek tragedy, staring down at their shoes as though they've just discovered their feet. When the doors open, they bolt like thoroughbreds from the starting gate. But no matter how awkward the situation, like Tammy Wynette, I stand by my man!

Once, when we were on a hospital elevator, your father stared at the silent little group for maybe fifteen seconds before blurting out, "Have you ever noticed how people on elevators clam up and avoid eye contact?"

One or two of them looked hopefully at the numbers above the door—the way drivers waiting at an intersection look at the traffic light, willing it to change before the guy with the collection bucket reaches their car. The rest began to check their iPhones and watches.

"Tough room," I whispered to Dad as we got off. I glanced back one last time and heard a man say to his wife, "Must be the psyche floor."

Sometimes I use a diversionary tactic when your father looks like he's about to speak to strangers. "I think I'm passing a kidney stone," I'll whisper, doubling over. Once, as he was opening his mouth to speak, I told him there was a bug crawling out of his ear. By the time he investigated, the doors opened, and his audience disappeared.

As you know, when he's involved in a play, Dad loves to practice his accents in public. Now he does so on elevators with a truly captive audience. Early one morning in a California hotel, we were alone and going down to breakfast when the doors opened and a lovely young lady in tennis shoes, sweatpants, and t-shirt joined us.

When your father took a deep breath, I knew what was coming. I lowered my head, covered my eyes, and groaned.

"Top o' the mornin' to ya, Lassie," he said. "And where might ye be headed on this bonny day?" She looked up from her smartphone as though she were being stalked by the Irish paparazzi. For a minute, I was afraid she was going to push the distress button on the panel and scream for help. But a second later, the door opened and, as she bounded off, she turned and said, "I'm going to the gym and spa. Have a good day." And all was right with the world.

Dad is currently studying lines for the role of Val, a Russian immigrant in Neil Simon's Laughter on the 23rd Floor. This morning after breakfast he said, "Vell, you vant I should go to store? Zee eggs and zee milk, zay are kaput." I don't mind his accents when we're alone. In fact, I find it kind of endearing.

It's a clear day, so this afternoon we're going to one of our favorite city destinations: the Inner Harbor, where we'll be visiting the observation deck of Baltimore's World Trade Center. It's a long ride to the top, and I'm worried people have had enough Russian interference.

Anyway, Mike, please tell your little Facebook friends that I'm very grateful for their interest in my book, and if they run into your father while waiting for an elevator, they should feel free to introduce themselves; he really is a lot of fun.

Then they should consider the stairs.

Love,
Mom

→ WHAT'S A WIFE FOR, ANYWAY? ←

*Y*ESTERDAY WAS WHAT STARTED OUT TO BE one of those leisurely mornings we seniors know all too well. But after breakfast, my husband left the table and minutes later returned with the portable landline and his broken laptop. With the phone on speaker, he dialed the toll-free number for technical support.

"I might as well get this over with. Maybe they can do something about this black screen," he said, sighing heavily. You would think he were scheduling an appointment for major surgery.

He made it sound like a chore, but I knew better. I topped off his coffee and prayed for a patient technician.

John is a friendly, yet endlessly curious man. I think of him as the Larry King of the Rowe family—except that, in his eighties, he's still on his first wife. One of his favorite pastimes since retiring is chatting with strangers—over coffee at McDonalds, in line at the grocery store, on an elevator . . . anyplace, really, where people aren't in a rush. He's especially partial to calls from telemarketers. Unlike most normal people, my husband waits for their calls, then pounces.

"So, tell me, Richard," he'll say, "is that your real name? Where are you calling from? Really! What's the weather like in Bangkok? How long have you been doing this? Do you work from home? Do you work on commission?"

My husband has never made a purchase over the phone—and he never will.

Once he called the 800 number on the back of a bag of SunChips and chatted for half an hour. "Hey, what's up with those loud, crinkly bags?" he began. "How's a guy supposed to sneak a few of his favorite chips without his wife hearing?"

John stared thoughtfully at the black screen of his ailing computer and waited.

"Customer Service. How can I help you?"

"Hello, young man! What sort of accent is that?"

"What is your name?"

"How do you spell that?"

By the time the dishwasher was loaded and the sink scoured, I knew enough about Jithin to write his biography. He lives in India and his native tongue is Hindi. Yes, he saw *Slum Dog Millionaire* and no, it was not a completely accurate depiction of his people.

Suddenly, John shouted, "Hey hon, look! You won't believe this!" He was waving his arms above his head as though he was trying to flag down a passing motorist, while his curser floated effortlessly across the screen like a kite on a March day.

"No hands! He's controlling my mouse all the way from Calcutta, India! Do you believe that?"

You'd have thought the guy was David Copperfield.

"If you ever lose this gig, young man, you can be a hacker," John told him, sounding like a high school career counselor—with questionable advice.

In case you're curious, Jithin is only twenty years old and a member of the Hindu faith. He believes in reincarnation, but he isn't sure he considers cows sacred.

"A lot of people in India do," John told him—in case he hadn't heard.

Following an interesting discussion of whirling dervishes, voilà! No more black screen.

Jithin's voice suddenly took on a businesslike tone. "Is there anything else I can help you with today, Mr. Rowe?"

"Um, did you see *Gandhi*? Wasn't Ben Kingsley amazing?" David Copperfield wasn't getting off this easy if my husband had anything to do with it.

It was sad to watch—like a fisherman who had been playing a marlin at the end of his line and realizing it was getting away.

I rushed to John's side, kissed his forehead, and whispered, "Why don't you ask Jithin why your computer is so slow, hon?" He smiled and winked at me.

What's a wife for, anyway?

→ IT'S ALL IN THE WRIST ←

Dear Michael,

*T*hank you for the crab cakes! Nothing says Merry Christmas quite like a dozen award-winning, frozen, jumbo lump crab cakes from Maryland's Eastern Shore. My mouth is watering just writing about them.

We had a nice Christmas. Your niece surprised Dad with a fitness tracker, which he immediately strapped to his wrist and wears as faithfully as he did his dog tags in Korea—even in the shower.

If yesterday is any indication of our future, I shall be quite mad by spring. Welcome to my world.

December 26, 8:00 a.m.

"Good morning, hon," your father said, still in bed and squinting at his left wrist. "Listen to this. I walked 900 steps just going to the bathroom last night. Imagine that!"

And no, Mike, he doesn't walk to the filling station on the corner. Let me explain. You know about old men and their prostates. Well, Dad gets a call from nature several times a night and has discovered that if he takes a few laps around the condo first, he has more immediate success, if you know what I mean. So every night while I'm sleeping, your father impersonates a guard on sentry duty. The neighbors probably think we're sleepwalkers. Or maybe they chalk it up to some kinky nighttime ritual.

December 26, 12:00 p.m.
Dad tapped his wrist and made a public service announcement: "It's 12 o'clock, the 26th of December, 2018. I'm taking out the trash and recycling."

December 26, 12:11 p.m.
Your father returned and looked yet again at his you-know-what. "That took exactly ten and a half minutes. I walked 300 steps and burned ten calories. How about that!"

"If you're expecting a standing ovation, you're wasting your time," I said. "I'm too busy." Sometimes it's hard to resist sarcasm.

December 26, 3:30 p.m.
"I'm off for my walk, hon." Dad checked his wrist and put on his radio headset. Then like some modern-day Jack LaLanne, he headed for the walking path, his arms swinging vigorously.

December 26, 4:33 p.m.
"I'm back!" he called. "I walked three miles in sixty-one minutes and burned 300 calories! Two-thousand steps per mile; 6,000 steps total. Not bad for eighty-five years of age, huh?" he said, sucking in and patting his stomach. (He does that a lot.) It's too bad that device doesn't measure the time he spends on the bathroom scales. He weighs himself more often than a jockey.

December 26, 11:15 p.m.
I was in bed while the energizer bunny sat at the desk waving his wrist above his computer. "Are you ready, hon?" (My heart used to skip a beat when I heard those words.) "I walked 11,500 steps today and burned at least 500 calories. We should get you one of these

things, Peg. They're amazing!"

"Right!"

"And listen to this: I had three hours of deep sleep last night, four hours of light sleep, and two hours of wakefulness." He was probably staring at his wrist for those two hours.

I had a moment of hope last week when the band around Dad's wrist fell apart. He went to Best Buy and got a wild new one. It's a girl's band, but I didn't tell him. It looks like he's wearing a Holstein cow around his wrist—or a composition notebook. Maybe he'll get tired of looking at it and take it off.

Love,
Mom

P.S. Your niece called today to see how the fitness tracker is working out. I told her Granddad loves it. (I didn't mention that it will probably land me in an institution.) Then she casually mentioned that there would be an addition to our family.

Apparently, she drove through a bad cell, and I lost her. I was dreaming of our first great-grandchild when she called back with the rest of the story. She and Mark are adopting a couple of pet rats.

Happy New Year, Mike!

⇾ THE FAMILY TABLE ⇽

*W*HEN IT COMES TO TV VIEWING, MY husband and I are polar opposites. If the expression, "You are what you watch" has any validity at all, John is an FBI agent, a coroner, a crime detective, or a forensics expert—who moonlights as a wildlife photographer. I'm a sheriff in the peaceful town of Mayberry, or a nobody who marries a prince on Hallmark.

The idea of watching a show with violence and blood and weapons makes me ill. "It's just pretend," John will say. "I don't know what you're so upset about. It's not really happening."

I say, "No, thank you"—although, for the sake of togetherness, I do make the occasional concession. I tried to join my husband for a story about a Northwest Passage expedition. I sat through deprivation, floggings, illness, mutiny, starvation, and a monstrous polar bear—but I drew the line at eating your best friend.

"This is history, hon," my husband will say. "It's reality; it really happened!"

To which I respond, "You know, going to the bathroom is reality. It really happens. But I'm not going to sit there and watch it."

To his credit, John will sit with me and watch the occasional feel-good show. Last week we saw *A Tree Grows in Brooklyn,* and he was hooked!

Even seemingly harmless nature shows can be upsetting. The other night my husband was in the living room watching a program on the Serengeti. When he called, "Hey, come look at this, hon!" I peeked cautiously around the corner, expecting to see lions fighting to the death over territory, crocodiles crunching down on their four-legged catch of the day, or wildebeests being savaged by hyenas—or cheetahs—or African wild dogs—or lions. It's never a good time to be a wildebeest.

My eyes immediately misted over at the peaceful, domestic scene before me. A family of big cats had gathered around their meal while the sun shone overhead, and golden Serengeti grasses waved in the background. Two fuzzy cubs played tug of war nearby while a third lapped lazily from a small puddle beside his parents.

"Aw," I said, putting on my glasses and sitting beside John on the sofa. "See hon? Even wild animals can enjoy the *family table.*"

———◆———

The dinner hour was sacred at our house. It was one of my few demands. I was nowhere near as controlling as my mother had been, but I did adhere to her thoughts about dinnertime and the family table. It was a time of togetherness where we shared the events of the day.

Telephone, television, and books were off limits at the dinner table. Fortunately, I didn't have to compete with electronics. I didn't get upset when I heard the term "television police," unless it came from my husband who routinely complained about missing the evening news while we ate. The cooking might not have been gourmet, but there were often candles, soft music in the background, and fresh flowers from the garden. My mother did teach me a thing or two about civilized dining.

At its best, dinnertime was laughter, kids throwing out one-liners, reciting a favorite poem, or John sharing an interesting story from the paper. Conversations could be revealing. During one such meal, a son shared that a half-dozen boys from his class had been kicked out of assembly that morning for booing the principal. He assured us he wasn't among them. It was at another such dinner where we learned that our fourteen-year-old son had a girlfriend and had been invited to a boy-girl party at her house that Saturday night. I made a point of remembering her name so that I could call her mother for details.

I admit that, despite good intentions, the dinner hour occasionally dissolved into chaos. Sometimes conversation amounted to *pumping* tight-lipped sons, with little more than a grunt for my effort. On those occasions, John would shoot me an accusatory look and remind me that, "We could be watching the evening news!"

At its worst, the family table was an indigestion-producing battlefield, with picky eaters, sibling rivalry, and a father critical of table manners.

But still, I held fast.

Things were going south quickly on the Serengeti. One of the adults growled menacingly. The other rose and backed away from what was, at closer inspection, a bloody, fly-covered carcass—but not before tearing off a chunk of dripping red flesh. The two cubs dropped their meaty bone, snarled, and pounced on each other, fighting to the death, it appeared. The third cub continued lapping from the puddle (which, when viewed up close, was bright red)—while several buzzards circled overhead.

"Remind you of anything, Peg?" John asked, laughing.

"I'm sure I don't know what you're talking about," I said, hurrying from the room.

———◆———

Things changed considerably when our children grew up and left home. Our current family table consists of TV trays in the living room and supper in front of the evening news programs. Actually, it's my favorite part of the day. Like a picnic with my best friend.

A picnic without flies—or blood—or buzzards.

→ BY THE SEAT OF HIS PANTS ←

*M*IKE WAS BARELY OUT OF COLLEGE WHEN he invested his pitiful savings on hundreds of household water filters. The fact that he had never even seen a water filter and hadn't a clue how they worked, did not deter him from selling them door-to-door.

For months, we lived like hoarders, sidestepping around boxes of water filters in our dining room and basement, while Mike squeezed into the driver's seat of a car that was packed with "inventory." Neither friends nor neighbors were safe from a spontaneous sales pitch. The boxes of water filters eventually disappeared—all sold. Nobody was more surprised than his parents.

Likewise, our son knew nothing about computers when he took a job with a national computer company. He confided in us that he did learn how to turn the computer on and off before his job began.

Then there were the years Mike hosted QVC. He flew by the seat of his pants for entire three-hour shifts, treating unfamiliar tools like old buddies, extolling the virtues of eighteen karat gold like a Tiffany salesman, and sounding like Martha Stewart as he discussed the thread count of sheets and pillowcases.

Watching Mike on QVC was better than having a front row seat at a comedy club. When he held up a Craftsmen wrench and used words like *tork* and *leverage* and *heft*, his father and I laughed, remembering Mike as a young homeowner. When something broke, he'd thrown up his hands and invited his dad and grandfather for a visit with the caveat, "Bring your toolbox along." He did invest in one tool—a paintbrush. When he finished painting his upstairs, he threw it away.

"As God is my witness," he vowed in a Scarlet O'Hara moment, "I'll work very hard at my craft, save my money, and hire somebody who knows what the heck he's doing, the next time!"

Except for a watch, Mike has never owned a piece of jewelry. Yet there he was on national television bejeweled in a chunky gold bracelet, a big ruby ring, and a Diamonique tie tack. I didn't recognize those manicured hands holding the sparkling gems.

Mike was in his glory whenever he shared the stage with a lovely model. There was a mischievous glint in his eye as he approached her with his centimeter ruler. Once, when things were slow in the wee hours of the morning, he measured the model's earring, and then, with laughter in the background, proceeded to measure her ear as she was undoubtedly rethinking her career choice. He was eyeing her nose when they broke for a commercial.

At least one person found Mike's performance with jewelry inspiring. Six-year-old Katie gave Uncle Mike her undivided attention as he talked at great length about Black Hills Gold and Diamonique pendants and earrings.

Adorned in my jangling bracelets, dangling earrings, and inexpensive beaded necklaces, our granddaughter produced, directed, and hosted her own show from our living room sofa, which she called *The Jewelry Jam*. With granddad manning the video camera, and my costume jewelry spread out before her on a black velvet scarf covering the coffee table, Katie offered up my treasures at bargain basement prices in three easy payments—plus shipping and handling, of course. Only my wedding rings and my genuine Mikimoto pearls were off-limits. My husband had sent the necklace home to his grandmother during the Korean War when he was stationed in Japan, and there was no way I was going to see this treasure offered for $3.35 in three easy payments.

Most entertaining of all was the way Mike reacted to collectable dolls, as if they were little aliens hurled to Earth from a spaceship. He just didn't get it and would have willingly sloshed through sewers to escape the little creatures. After gleaning and sharing every scrap of information from the blue card that accompanied each product, he was still at a loss—every second, agonizing—with two minutes to go before a break. I knew he was desperate when he began playing with the doll's white cotton socks.

"And this . . ." he told his audience, as though he was about to share a secret cure for psoriasis, "is an option you have. You can pull her little white socks up to her knees, or you can fold them down, just so. She can wear them up—or she can wear them down."

Eventually, as the hour wore on, out of pure desperation, he resorted to making up stories, placing the dolls in edgy scenarios, or singing rhyming ditties about them—not always appropriate. Once he referred to the twinkle in a doll's eye that hinted of a checkered past and suggested that viewers would be shocked if they knew her secrets.

"Don't be fooled by that innocent little smile," he warned. When dolls routinely sold out, I realized I wasn't the only one being entertained. Unbeknownst to me at the time, Mike's middle-of-the-night humor had gained him a cult-like following, especially on the West Coast, as well as devoted insomniacs in the Central and Eastern time zones.

Ideally, hosts would come to work early to preview the products beforehand. We could always tell by his deer-in-the-headlights look when Mike wasn't prepared. Watching him claw his way to the surface was agonizing for me but great fun for his father, who would talk to his son, saying something like, "Uh huh . . . the adrenaline's pumping now, isn't it, son?"

One night, Mike looked up to see a set of four heavy oak TV trays stacked on a sturdy wooden stand and was visibly impressed. After solving the mystery of how to set them up, he raved about how *solid* they were.

"These rugged tables would be at home in any man cave or clubroom during say, the Super Bowl or the World Series." He went so far as to compare them to inferior models. "You've seen them," he said with disdain. "Flimsy metal legs with cheap plastic snap-on trays." He had the decency not to add, "Like the ones in my parents' house." We had gotten them with Green Stamps years before.

His presentation was creative and masterful. "I'm seeing a roomful of macho guys—a huge platter of wings on this tray and some footlongs on that one."

Sales were brisk, and in no time a Sold Out banner flashed across the screen.

When the product coordinators carried in the next item, Mike froze. I moaned when I saw the set of four cheap plastic TV trays snapped onto flimsy metal legs.

Ordinarily, Mike pulled late night shifts but on this particular day he was filling in for a popular primetime host who had the flu. Millions were watching. I was excited for him and, along with my mother, had speculated on who might be among the viewers— the president, diplomats, famous writers, movie stars. . . .

My husband slapped his knee and howled, then pointed to our identical trays in the corner. "Let's see what you do with this one, Einstein—after you take your foot out of your mouth! Ha, ha, ha!"

As usual, within seconds, Mike recovered, saying something like, "Do you have kids? Because if you do, these are great! See?" he said, lifting the set of trays above his head with one hand. "They're light enough for anyone to handle, and at this price, you can afford a set for every room in the house. And look how easy they are to set up," he said, quickly arranging the four tables around him. He had been setting up our identical trays at home for years and could have done it in his sleep.

"You gotta give it to him," said John, shaking his head and smiling with pride. "The boy can talk!"

The night our son actually dozed off on the set of a QVC bedroom *on air*, I worried that he was sleep deprived. I was watching in the middle of the night from my living room as he demonstrated different bedding—linens, duvets, blankets, and so on. With soothing music playing softly in the background, Mike lay quietly on a mattress for a moment or so as callers placed orders. He later denied to me that he was actually asleep, but I could tell by the drool in the corner of his mouth. A mother knows.

The morning our son was advertising cookware and preparing an omelet, he suddenly dropped the frying pan and shook his hand. As it clattered onto the stove, he said calmly, "Whatever you do, don't touch that little piece of metal on the handle; it gets hot!" Following a commercial, Mike returned wearing a bulky white bandage on his finger. I felt physically ill.

To his credit, Mike uttered no expletives. (I can't say the same for his mother.) I still use my QVC purchases: a set of ceramic canisters on the kitchen counter, some T-fal cookware (I'm careful not to touch that little piece of metal on the handle of the frying pan), and a set of sturdy wooden TV trays. (Yeah, I fell for the pitch.)

For me, Mike's most memorable and exciting QVC appearances were when he hosted three holiday specials with Joan Rivers—*prime time*! The fact that she had specifically requested my son to be her host, in my mind, catapulted him to the pinnacle of the entertainment industry—well, the home shopping industry anyway. When he told me that *the* Joan Rivers had invited him to a Christmas party at her fancy NYC apartment, I went weak in the knees. When I recovered, I asked,

"So, Mike, what will you be taking to the party as a hostess gift?" Because in my world, no one attends a party empty-handed.

He said the unthinkable. "Nothing. Mom, Joan Rivers doesn't need a thing!"

We all know that it isn't about need, so I took care of it. A week later Mike boarded a train for New York City carrying a festive holiday tin filled with his mother's homemade chocolate chip cookies under his arm.

Late that evening, I smiled as I imagined Joan and Melissa sitting in front of a fire with their feet up enjoying cookies and a glass of milk while the "help" cleared away the mess around them. It's what I would have done.

⟫◆⟪

I always felt that Mike's destiny at QVC was clinched one Sunday afternoon in December. It was an hour of Christmas toys, and though his experience with children was limited, Mike's inner child enjoyed riding little trucks around the set and building impressive structures with blocks.

His unfortunate revelation came as he was chatting with a caller. It went something like this: "I still remember when I learned there was no Santa Claus. It's one of those moments you never forget. How old were you when you realized there was no Santa Claus?"

Poor Mike. How was he supposed to know that the afternoon audience for an hour of children's Christmas toys would be comprised largely of children looking at Christmas toys?

Within seconds, switchboards were ablaze with irate parents—all out for poor Mike's hide.

It was inevitable. A person can fly by the seat of his pants for only so long!

→ OLD BLUE ←

Michael,

*I*t's your mother. You seem very busy here of late, writing stories and sharing them with your little friends on Facebook. Perhaps that's why I've heard nothing from you after leaving several messages over the weekend. If you'd prefer that we communicate publicly, I'm happy to do so through a series of short stories posted on our respective Facebook pages. Unfortunately, I have no idea how to post a video, but if I did, I'd record and post this account of my adventure over the weekend. It needs a title, and I'm stuck between "Old Blue" and "Walmart People." I'll let you decide.

You know that I am a responsible person. Not once did I forget to pick up you or your brothers after ball practice or Boy Scouts. Not once did I leave your elderly grandparents at the mall or forget to give them their medication. I've never run out of the house and left the stove on, or forgotten to turn off the iron, or even locked my keys in the car. And yet, somehow, I managed to leave my big blue purse dangling from the handle of a shopping cart in the Walmart parking lot. And frankly, I'm not sure I'll ever be the same.

I realized it was gone when I pulled into our parking spot at the condo yesterday and reached over into the passenger seat. Nothing. There are only so many places a big blue purse can hide in a Scion xB, and I checked them all. I also lifted the floor mats and opened the tiny glove compartment. Had there been an ashtray, I probably would have searched there as well.

I don't think I've felt this degree of anguish since that day in Kansas City while listening to you speak to a few hundred cancer survivors. Suddenly, out of the blue, you said to the crowd, "And now my mother, Peggy Rowe, would like to say a few words." I had considered passing out to teach you a lesson, but by the time I reached the podium, I had resumed breathing, and the nausea had passed. Mostly.

Anyway, I was sick with panic, but thankfully, your father had just returned from his Meals on Wheels obligations and was there with his soothing brand of logic and unflappable calm.

"John, I lost my big blue purse at Walmart!" I blurted, near tears.

"What?! You tossed your figs in a hearse that won't start?" I handed him his hearing aids and repeated.

"Oh no," he said. "This is terrible! Where did you last have it? When did you last see it? What exactly was in it?"

A dozen questions later, Perry Mason whipped out his flip phone and began canceling credit cards as I wept on a landline with Walmart Customer Service. There were no purses in lost and found, but Security promised to check around and call me back. Ten minutes later they did. No purses to be found—big, blue, or otherwise.

Meanwhile, your father began a written inventory of missing items: a $400 smartphone, my new prescription glasses, my favorite Timex watch (now with a brand-new Walmart battery), my driver's license, medical cards, gift cards, cash. ....Then he suddenly threw down the pen and jumped up.

"Come on, Peg. We're going back to that parking lot. Maybe somebody just took the cash and threw everything else away. Crooks do that, you know."

"Do they, John? Do crooks linger in the Walmart parking lot inspecting the contents of stolen purses, deciding what to keep and what to discard at a civilized and leisurely pace?"

Your father, immune to sarcasm, was already out the door and halfway down the stairs, hell-bent on retrieving what was rightfully ours.

"You can't go out dressed in those ratty old clothes!" I called after him—but of course, he could and he did. And fifteen minutes later, after a white-knuckle ride through five miles of rush hour traffic, we were parked in the same spot I had vacated an hour earlier.

Dad jumped from the car and ran to the cart corral, where he conducted a quick but fruitless inspection of every cart. Then he proceeded to a nearby trashcan, removed the lid, and peered inside. Dressed in his Dirty Jobs t-shirt and a pair of Bermuda shorts from 1979, he appeared ready to scrounge for his next meal. But food was the last thing on your father's mind, as he cranked his hearing aids to the "stethoscope" setting, pulled out his flip phone, dialed my smartphone, and plunged his head into the garbage can.

Call me snooty, Mike, but it's hard to stand by while your husband dumpster dives at the local Walmart.

"I'm going inside to check with Security," I yelled, above the din of passing cars. "Don't be surprised if people stop and offer you change." But he didn't hear me.

As I crossed the vast blacktop toward the sprawling super center, I passed a number of Walmart shoppers heading for their cars. Which of these fine citizens, I wondered, might have stumbled across my big blue purse and returned it to Lost and Found? The pale girl dressed in black with the metal dog collar around her neck? The shirtless gentleman with a leather vest and a Mohawk? Maybe the young couple with matching nose rings and tattoos on their foreheads?

My shoulders were slumped as I reached the store. But on the positive side, I could see Dad was, in fact, far from underdressed. Before entering, I glanced back to monitor your father's progress. He had made it halfway across the parking lot, one can at a time—tap,

tap, tapping his little flip phone and cocking his head to the side like an Irish Setter, listening for signs of life in the garbage. No luck, obviously.

Inside, I located the Lost and Found, which consisted of an assortment of mismatched mittens, scarves, baby bottles, and paci-fiers—but no purses. "Excuse me," I said, "Is there a manager I can speak with?"

"Try register 20," the harried worker said with a shrug. "Sometimes the manager hangs out there."

There was no manager at register 20, but as I spoke with the cashier, I heard in the near distance a familiar sound—the classic ring of an ancient telephone unrecognizable to anyone born in this century—my custom ring tone. Heart racing, I followed the sound to a shelf off to the side of the register, and there, surrounded by a mishmash of odds and ends, was my big blue purse, peering out at me like ET from a cluttered closet. I pounced on it, kissed it, and took out my phone, which was still ringing. It was John.

"John," I said, projecting my voice as I usually do when speaking to your father. "Guess what?!"

"Geez, stop shouting!" he said. "I know! You found it! Come out front; I want you to meet somebody." I left the store clutching my purse to my heart. By that time, I had affectionately named it "Old Blue."

A woman sitting behind the wheel of a car was laughing with Dad—or possibly at him.

"Hey Peg, this lady found your purse and took it in to Security. I thought you might want to thank her."

Her name was Beverly, and she had been intrigued by the sight of an elderly man in the parking lot, running from trashcan to trashcan, dialing his phone, then sticking his head inside the receptacle.

Instead of calling 911 to report a Silver Alert or taking his picture to submit to People of Walmart, Beverly called out to him from her car.

"Are you looking for something, sir?"

"Yes! I'm looking for a big blue purse!"

"Ahh, I turned it in an hour ago. I found it hanging from the handle of a shopping cart right over there."

I wanted to kiss the woman, but some people are funny about being kissed by strangers. So, we chatted for a moment, and I told her how foolish I felt and how careless I had been.

"Oh, that's nothing," said Beverly. "One day I came home from shopping, opened my trunk, and it was empty. I had left all of my groceries in the cart at the store."

We all had a good laugh, and when your father offered her a gift, she said, "No, no, I won't take a thing. Just seeing the look on your faces is reward enough."

Anyway Mike, I'm not sure there's a moral to this story beyond the fact that you never know who you're going to meet at Walmart. Your father might have another interpretation, but I'll let you ask him about that this evening when you call us after dinner. In the meantime, if you share this story with your little friends on Facebook, don't mention Beverly's name. I'd hate to embarrass her. In fact, don't mention mine, either, or our phone numbers, which I've attached for your convenience.

Talk soon,
Mom

P.S. What kind of person forgets to put their groceries into the trunk? I mean, really. . . .

→ WHAT'S A MOTHER TO DO? ←

I DON'T REMEMBER EXACTLY WHEN IT happened—my transition from anxious, overprotective mother to world-weary showbiz mom. I just know that when I turned on the television one night and saw my firstborn stripped to the waist and standing in fresh manure with his arm up the rear end of a bull, I didn't reach for a Valium. I merely shook my head and wondered for the hundredth time, *Where did I go wrong?*

———◆———

It was the retirement most couples dream about. We had sold our house of forty years and moved into a condominium—no weeds to whack or grass to cut, no dead branches to trim, or snow to shovel. Our three grown sons were on their own, and we were enjoying the pleasures of life.

Then came *Dirty Jobs*.

John and I sat in front of the television that first Tuesday night like two wide-eyed children in front of the tree on Christmas morning. When the phone rang, I knew just who it was.

"Hi Mom," I said, glancing at the clock.

My mother was actually giggling. "Are you watching? It's one minute before nine," she said.

"Yes, Mom, we're watching; I'll call you after the show."

"Isn't this exciting," she said before hanging up.

The *record* light flashed on the VCR, soda fizzed in our glasses, and the aroma of buttered popcorn filled the den.

We smiled proudly as the opening credits flashed on the screen and Mike's name appeared beside the quirky title of the show he had created for Discovery Channel. Finally! After twenty years of selling everything from water filters and magazines, to computer maintenance contracts and jewelry on late night TV, our boy had made the big time. I reached out and held John's hand remembering Mike's long journey through local theater and TV commercials, the opera, several marginally successful TV series, and those endless infomercials. At last! A respectable show on a highly rated cable network.

Suddenly, there he was—our son—or so we were led to believe. He was wearing protective clothing and standing knee-deep in guano, surrounded by blackness and deadly fumes. As urine and other bodily fluids from millions of bats rained from above, a biologist warned Mike that the guano was filled with dermestid beetles committed to cleaning the flesh from his bones if given half a chance.

At the first commercial break, my husband and I turned to each other, numb, our mouths open, the soda and popcorn untouched.

The night Mike donned a rubber suit and descended into the city sewers, I kept my eyes shut. No mother should have to watch rats the size of Yorkshire terriers running over her son's legs and giant roaches violating his body. The day he worked in a charcoal pit, his father screamed at him, "Put on a mask, son! What's wrong with you?"

I used to travel our neighborhood walking path in relative anonymity, but since *Dirty Jobs*, people shouted to me from their balconies:

"Mike was at the dump again last night, Peggy! He must smell like rotten garbage."

Or, "Saw your son getting very personal with an alligator."

The week after Mike worked side by side with a Montana rancher castrating lambs the old-fashioned way—with his teeth—I took my walks after dark.

With each episode of *Dirty Jobs*, I was filled with wonder—and sometimes horror. How does someone born into a middle-class family in the suburbs of Baltimore smile as he's sloshing through human waste or make jokes while he's straddling a 500-pound sow during artificial insemination? The night I saw my son meticulously combing hippopotamus poo from his hair, I marveled that the adult on the screen was such a contrast to the child I nurtured.

I can still see that toddler in a high chair, waving his hands after every bite and demanding, "Wash sticky fingers!"

When I learned how many millions of people worldwide were watching Discovery Channel's *Dirty Jobs,* I remembered the shy kid who dove beneath the kitchen table or made a beeline for the hall closet every time the doorbell rang. "I don't want people to look at me," he would explain quietly. I used to lie awake nights envisioning my child's future as a pitiful recluse.

Mike's amazing transformation came at Overlea High School. "I got the lead in the senior play," he mentioned at dinner one evening. He said it in the same voice he might have used to say, "Please pass the potatoes."

"What's the matter?" Mike asked, when his father and I stared dumbly.

"Uh . . . can we come?" I asked.

"Sure. Anybody can come. It's called *Oklahoma!*"

My husband and I sat close together in the school auditorium chewing our fingernails on opening night.

"Surely, they wouldn't let him do this if he weren't capable," John said. We were dizzy from holding our breath by the time the curtain rose and a rich, deep voice floated from the wings.

"There's a bright golden haze on the meadow . . ."

We were dumbfounded. Was this really the same ten-year-old kid who refused to walk into Boy Scouts that first night because he didn't want all those strangers to look at him? We sat through every performance, mesmerized, and before long were following our son's show business career.

There were community theater productions, barbershop quartet and chorus performances, and local TV commercials. When Mike joined the Baltimore Opera, two parents who didn't know the difference between *Sweeney Todd* and *The Barber of Seville* didn't miss a performance.

When Mike became a host on QVC in the early 1990s, we subscribed to cable TV. I set the alarm and sat in my pajamas drinking tea from 3:00 a.m. to 6:00 a.m. several times a week. My husband questioned my sanity.

"Only a mother," he would say, rolling over in bed. I watched my boy on national TV hawking merchandise he knew nothing about. The night he dozed off in front of millions of viewers while demonstrating bedding, I worried that he was sleep-deprived. At least he didn't snore.

I thought of those safe QVC days that night on *Dirty Jobs* when a snake sank his fangs into our son's wrist, then dangled from his arm. I don't know what's around the corner for Mike professionally, or for us—his most avid fans. I do know that I was especially proud of myself the night he was in a sewer with rats and roaches scampering over his body. I remained calm and didn't cover my eyes once. My son hopped around the sewer as the workers laughed at him and I thought back to a Saturday morning long ago.

Mike was a teenager and helping his brothers stack firewood when he noticed a nest of young mice embedded in a log. He carried the piece of wood to the backyard and tapped it hard against the ground. Sure enough, a litter of baby mice emerged, and, following their instincts, immediately shot up my son's pant leg to a dark and safe space.

I was nearly as frantic as Mike as he whooped and hollered, dancing around the yard. "Somebody help him!" I yelled. Family and neighbors laughed hysterically when he dropped his jeans and pulled a young mouse from his crotch. Then another . . . then another.

None of us realized at the time that Mike was in training for *Dirty Jobs* and would one day be doing this dance on national television.

→ WE'RE KEEPING HIM ←

*W*HEN FANS OF *DIRTY JOBS* LEARN THAT WE'RE
Mike Rowe's parents, they usually stare for a few seconds
before asking which one of us Mike takes after.

This question always makes me laugh.

In the second season of the show, Mike jumped into a school
of thrashing sharks in the Caribbean. I won't get into a swimming pool if kids are splashing. In Michigan, Mike climbed eight
hundred feet above the water to change a light bulb at the top of
the Mackinac Bridge. I need a Dramamine® to look down from
our second-floor balcony.

It's hard to believe Mike has my genes. I've even entertained
the possibility of some baby mix-up in the hospital nursery all
those years ago.

"Oh," the people say, "so Mike must take after his father."

This is funnier, still. Mike Rowe's resume boasts of more than
300 jobs since college. His father taught in the same classroom for
thirty years. Mike's address appears only in pencil in my address
book and has been erased so many times there's a hole in the paper.
We lived in the same house for forty years before moving into our
condominium.

Mike, who is famous for his spontaneous, impetuous nature,
grew up with a father who is a slave to excruciating detail.

On road trips, a notebook and a calculator are as essential to my husband as air in the tires and gasoline in the fuel tank. Entries are my responsibility; I write nonstop—departure and arrival times, distance between towns, time and duration at rest stops, miles-per-gallon calculations at gas stations, and locations of restaurants and motels. When we arrive home after our adventure, John raves over the beautiful mountains, the black bear with her cute cub near the side of the road, a lovely sunrise . . . I don't know what he's talking about. I completely missed Georgia on our drive to Florida last year.

On one visit to San Francisco, Mike took us sightseeing. When he pulled into a gas station, John asked, "Do they have the best price? Where does this gas come from? Does it contain ethanol? Is this where you usually get gas, son?"

Mike smiled patiently and looked at his father for a second. "See that little red needle, Dad?" he said, pointing to the dashboard. "When it gets close to the E, I fill her up at the next station."

John's jaw dropped at such an offhand remark. I marveled at the simplicity of it all—pulling into a gas station, filling the tank, and taking the highway. No entries in a notebook, no calculators, and no exclamations over good or bad mileage. I could get used to that!

On Mike's last visit home, he commented on the poor quality of the TV in our bedroom.

"The picture is shrinking," he informed me.

"Oh, we know," I said. "We have to get a new one. Your father has been doing his exhaustive research." I pointed to a yellow legal pad on John's desk, covered with numbers and calculations. "You know your father!"

Mike laughed, being well acquainted with his father's compulsion. After lunch, he disappeared and returned an hour later carrying a brand-new television.

"What do you mean, you just bought it?" John asked, scratching his head. "Nobody *just buys* a television! Did you do comparison shopping? How do you know this is a good product? Did you check *Consumer Reports*? Where are your notes? Did you have a coupon?"

I laughed. My husband is the only shopper salespeople do not pounce on. Quite the contrary; they scatter like roaches at sunrise when he enters their department. You'd think he was carrying a flamethrower instead of a harmless yellow legal pad.

Mike smiled and put his arm around his father's shoulder. "It's a top brand, Dad. You'll love it." Before John could utter the word "extravagant," our son added, *"And I'm not taking it back!"*

To this day, my husband shakes his head when he looks at that TV—a monument to the baffling, impetuous nature of his oldest son.

From time to time, John still ponders the baby mix-up-in-the-nursery theory, but I can't really buy that. Having a 9½-pound baby with a, shall we say, prominent head is among my more vivid memories.

Whatever, we're keeping him.

→ POO-DINI ←

A WOMAN APPROACHED ME AT A SOCIAL gathering and asked if it was true that I was the mother of that *Dirty Jobs* guy. I said that I was and braced myself for the usual glowing praise. I had gotten used to people telling me they loved my son—his message, his show, his voice, his looks . . .

"Tell him I said thanks," she said, a little too vehemently. "My three-year-old grandson says poop every other minute of the day! I can't take him out in public!" She rolled her eyes and walked away, muttering, "Thank you, thank you, thank you."

Since *Dirty Jobs* began, our son has been on intimate terms with poop from every imaginable source—or as he puts it, "feces from every species"—elephant, giraffe, penguin, dog, cow, horse, pig, bat, worm, pigeon, alligator, snake, monkey, lemur, and human.

At the conclusion of an episode where Mike had cleaned the hippopotamus pool at a zoo, my husband turned to me with that long-suffering expression. "Just another ordinary Tuesday night at home watching a grown son comb hippopotamus poop from his hair."

In reality, we felt blessed. The previous Tuesday we had watched him reach into the rear end of a cow and pull fists full of fetid fecal matter from her bowels, commenting, "Holy crap!"

I grew up in a family of puritans where expletives like "Oh, shucks!" and "Darn it to heck" were considered crude. On rare occasions, Dad would paint the air blue with, "Go to war, Miss Agnes!" but was always contrite afterwards. My sister and I knew better than to say "shut up" or to utter the mother of all bad words: *fart*. In our house it was *gas*. Of course, with little ones, certain bathroom expressions were inevitable, even in my parents' home. Those words were *tee-tee* and *tu-tu*. Certainly, nothing as vulgar as *pee* or *poop* or—God forbid—*crap* was ever uttered in our home.

When I married a veteran, who had most recently shared a college dorm with dozens of men, my vocabulary horizons expanded a tad. Still, there was no salty language or bathroom talk in our house, especially in the presence of our three sons.

When a *Dirty Jobs* fan joked that her family refers to Mike as "Poo-Dini" and asked if Mike has always had a fascination for poop, I gave it serious thought. Were we in any way to blame for our son's romancing of poop on national television? Maybe those standing ovations for success during his potty training weren't such a good idea after all.

Actually, young Mike had a healthy disdain for the stuff. Whenever I changed his baby brothers' smelly diapers, he vanished like Cinderella at the stroke of midnight.

With one exception . . .

During one of my daily self-indulgences—an entire minute of privacy in the bathroom—our one-year-old reached through the playpen bars and feasted on dozens of big brother Mike's colorful plastic Tiddlywinks. (For the record, four-year-olds are rotten babysitters.) I like to think he did not intentionally feed the colorful pieces to his baby brother.

When the Tiddlywinks could not be accounted for, I panicked and rushed the baby to the pediatrician. He advised us that an X-ray was not an option as plastic would not be detected. But he did assure us that our one-year-old's digestive tract was equal to the challenge. The following day, after heaping helpings of mashed potatoes, our little Michelangelo presented us with the first of two unique sculptures. Young Mike was both repulsed and captivated by the incredible, vibrant spectacle in his brother's pants. It was the aurora borealis of bowel movements, and he obsessed over just one more glimpse. He simply couldn't get enough!

There were more mashed potatoes. Then, the following day, with big brother hovering like a helicopter on a rescue mission, it happened again—another brown miracle mass infused with blue, green, red, and yellow flecks, like a giant M&M-laced peanut butter cookie. This did not have an adverse effect on Mike. Indeed, it was quite the opposite, leaving our four-year-old with a rapt expression reminiscent of Bernadette of Lourdes. Of course, Bernadette's encounter led to sainthood, whereas Mike's resulted in something a bit less dramatic. He gave up Tiddlywinks—for good. Kind of like I gave up orange juice as a child after it had been laced with castor oil and forced down my throat.

Dirty Jobs poop continues to touch me in a personal way. It's not just the little flowerpot on the dining room sideboard Mike made from cow poop and sent me for my birthday, or the books he picked up for me on his travels. One was called *Everybody Poops* and examined waste from a wide variety of species. It was both revolting and hilarious. The other one was an exhaustive study of scat and tracks in Yellowstone called *Who Pooped in the Park?* Fun books for sure, and though they were basically for kids, I kept them on the living room coffee table as a reminder of our son's devotion to his parents.

One evening when I was out for a walk, my cell phone rang, and it was Mike. He and the crew had just left a child-care center where he had spent the day changing poopy diapers.

"I just wanted to thank you, Mom," he said, "for all the dirty diapers you changed. I don't know how you did it!"

"How nice," I said. "It's always gratifying to know that your kids think about you!"

Actually, I had been thinking about Mike too. I'd just stepped around a little pile of poo on the sidewalk.

I didn't mention it.

→ OLD BLUE—THE FOLLOW-UP ←

Hey Mike,

I was in the cereal aisle at the grocery store the other day, when a woman half my age ran up to me and pointed at Old Blue.

"You take that purse off that cart handle right now, young lady! You don't want to lose it again!" she said. I had no idea who she was, but we both had a good laugh before she walked away—and I promptly hung the strap around my neck.

Honestly, Mike, it's like leaving the house with George Clooney draped over my shoulder. People can't get enough of it. When a story is read by 100 million people, I guess there's bound to be some fallout.

Perhaps you and your little Facebook friends would like to hear some follow-up to my "Old Blue" story. Mostly it has been fun—like the morning I was signing in for my annual mammogram screening and secretaries ran to the window asking, "Is that Old Blue, Mrs. Rowe?" It wasn't quite as much fun later when the phlebotomist was so excited over meeting my big blue purse that she missed my big blue vein—twice! Fortunately, this isn't the year for my colonoscopy.

At the Lyric Opera House last Saturday night, your fans chanted "Old Blue, Old Blue," When I stood up and waved, they were visibly disappointed to see my small black purse, (which, by the way, matched my dressy black shoes).

"I'm president of the Old Blue Fan Club," one young woman told me. Do you think she was serious?

My favorite comment on your Facebook page, which your father read aloud, was from a woman who had loaded her grocery bags into the back of her pickup, then proceeded to the drive-through carwash. This made me feel a little better.

Here's the good news: after trying for weeks to track down the hero of my story, we finally found Beverly's phone number.

"Oh, I remember you," she said when I called. "I've been telling my Walmart story to everybody I know!"

And here's the bad news: Beverly had never heard of Mike Rowe—or Dirty Jobs…or Somebody's Gotta Do It…or Returning the Favor…or The Way I Heard It. I wasn't going to tell you this, but Dad says I should because it will keep you humble. So I told Beverly about the story on your Facebook page and waited while she brought it up on her computer.

And here's some more good news: "Oh I remember him!" she said. "He used to advertise real estate here in Baltimore. I watched him on Sunday mornings!"

Today, your father and I visited our Walmart hero—with a Friendly's gift card in hand—because Beverly and George have eleven grandchildren. And who doesn't like ice cream, right?

As one would expect, she's a nice lady and had us giggling as she related her side of the Walmart saga with high drama.

"I always park toward the back of the lot because I don't want any dings in my car—it's kind of new. I spotted it right off: a blue pocket-book hanging on the handle of a cart in the corral."

Then she got real theatrical. "I looked all around and didn't see anybody, but I was afraid to touch it. I thought, What if she's loading her car and turns around to see me taking her purse? I don't want to get hit over the head! When nobody came, I picked it up and took it to Lost and Found."

Beverly demonstrated how she had nervously carried it away from her body so that her intentions to turn it in would be perfectly clear, in case she ran into the owner.

An hour later, this model citizen returned to her car, where, this time, she remembered to put her bags in the trunk!

"It was then I looked up and noticed an older gentleman wandering from trash can to trash can, sticking his head inside," she said. "I watched for a minute or two, trying to figure out what he was doing."

When she finished retelling the story, we took some pictures together, and Beverly wondered if we might like to get one of your father looking into the trash cans in her garage. Dad declined, graciously.

Beverly wants your Facebook friends to know that she doesn't make a habit of leaving $180 worth of groceries behind in parking lots. She had been distracted by a phone call. (At least that's her story, bless her heart.)

You gotta love Beverly!

Love,
Mom

P.S. What exactly did you mean by passive/aggressive in your video? If it means I take you for granted, you're mistaken. I cherish each and every one of your monthly phone calls.

Mike. Just had bizarre encounter at grocery store. A woman my age rushed up to me. "Oh Mrs. Rowe, I just adore your book! I can relate to you! The wrinkles, the gray hair—and I've put on a little weight around the middle just like you." She laughed. I'm used to people reminding me to take Old Blue off cart handle, but really Mike! This celebrity thing might be getting out of hand! Mom

⇢ IMPOSTERS IN TINSELTOWN ⇠

Y HUSBAND AND I SAT HUDDLED TOGETHER in the backseat of a black luxury car. Like two teenagers on their first date ever, we were filled with anticipation, excitement, and fear of the unknown.

Our chauffer maneuvered around several long luxury trailers before pulling to the curb in front of a white, two-story house in an upscale neighborhood in Pasadena, California. It was the kind of house you might drool over in magazines while imagining the occupants. John and I turned to each other, mouths open, and wide-eyed.

"What have you gotten us into?" my husband asked, congested from a head cold and breathing through his mouth. He always says that when he feels out of his element.

Like that time I had talked him into attending immersive theater. We found ourselves seated awkwardly in a large bathroom in a private home, while a nude actress recited a monologue from her bathtub. Fortunately, she was up to her neck in bubbles. I hoped she hadn't seen John glare at me or heard his whispered accusatory tone, "What have you gotten us into?"

Then there were the numerous operas John had reluctantly attended with my mother and me—because his son would be onstage. And that barbershop convention where we were subjected to woodshedding quartettes in lobbies, hallways, elevators, lavatories, and sidewalks.

The activity around this house in Pasadena was reminiscent of the hustle and bustle of roustabouts setting up a circus in The Greatest Show on Earth®.

In the driveway, craft services were cooking omelets to order and filling long tables with an exquisite breakfast buffet. Nearby, crew members were placing large, silver reflecting screens outside the windows of the house, attaching colorful artificial flowers to bushes, tying branches of greenery into trees, and carrying furniture and rolled up rugs from the house onto the lawn.

A young, energetic woman wearing a headset and carrying a clipboard met our car at the curb. "Hi," she said, "I'm Cindy. I'll be your handler for the day, and this is Josh, your personal assistant. If you need anything at all, just tell Josh."

The handsome young man was Hollywood personified, with a day's growth of beard and a casual, laid-back demeanor—a young wannabe performing menial tasks while waiting for his big break. I was wondering just what sort of service this assistant could offer us when Cindy said, "Are you hungry? Breakfast is over there in the driveway. They have anything you want." I had just opened my mouth to say, "I'd love a tall, decaf, fat-free latte" when Josh and John made a hasty retreat toward the driveway.

Cindy smiled. "Great. We'll just get you started with makeup and wardrobe, Mrs. Rowe."

What had I gotten us into indeed, I thought as I followed my handler to a long trailer.

———⟞◆⟝———

When *Dirty Jobs* became a hit on the Discovery Channel, my husband and I took on a new identity. No longer just John and Peggy Rowe, we were now "the parents of that dirty guy"—the one who scraped up roadkill, wiped pigeon poop from city window ledges, and sloshed through sewers and wastewater.

The first time I was introduced as "The Dirty Mother," I was shocked and maybe just a tad offended. It sounded unsavory somehow—a commentary on my character and hygiene. But it always got a big laugh, so I sucked it up and went along. When people talked about my son cleaning out septic tanks or emptying porta potties, I'd smile good-naturedly and remind them that someone gets up every morning to do those important jobs.

John and I had no sooner adjusted to our roles as parents of the "ambassador of dirt," when Mike threw us a curve. It was during a Sunday evening phone call, and he was on speaker.

"How would you guys like to come to California and do some filming?" he asked.

"What, us? Be in show business?" I asked. I didn't know what to think. Like most people of my generation, certain images of Hollywood are etched in my brain. Suddenly I was Deborah Kerr being swept around the palace dance floor in a long, flowing evening gown. . . . Then I was standing on a mountaintop in Austria singing "The Hills Are Alive." And I have to say, I liked it. But maybe Mike had something more dramatic in mind. Images of Rhett Butler carrying Scarlett O'Hara up a winding staircase flashed before me.

But then I remembered Janet Leigh being stabbed in a shower.

I was jolted back to reality by John's voice. "Mike, your mother and I are no longer in our prime. Besides, what could we do in a film? Certainly not sing or dance. I've done a lot of local theater, but nothing professional. And we don't look like those people you see in the movies. You know your mother has put on a few pounds and has those arthritic hands!"

Hmm . . . I started to remind my husband of his squeaky foot brace and whistling, ineffective hearing aids, but was interrupted.

"I'm not talking about a movie," our son said. "I'm talking about television—a commercial—the three of us. You guys could hang out in LA with me for a few days. How would you like that?"

"Hmm . . . Hang out where, Mike?" his father asked. "The Los Angeles dump? The La Brea Tar Pits? A sewage treatment plant?"

"The zoo?" I chimed in. Oh yeah, we were faithful viewers of *Dirty Jobs*.

That's when Mike informed us that Kimberly-Clark wanted us to do a commercial campaign for Viva paper towels. "You'll love it," he promised. "It's a big deal. Oh, and you'll be paid!"

"Count us in!" John yelled into the phone, a broad smile covering his face.

Naturally we accepted the offer, not just because we would be paid or because I actually used Viva paper towels, but because who could pass up a trip to Hollywood and the chance to work with the kid who had moved thousands of miles from home?

So with more than a little trepidation, two long in the tooth, slightly out-of-shape former educators who had never stood before a movie camera, stepped into a big, black car outside our Baltimore condo, waved goodbye to well-wishing neighbors, and headed off to the legendary Tinsel Town—via first class seats on United Airlines. It was like stepping onto the moon for the first time. I admit to feeling self-conscious when we were served warm mixed nuts and ginger ale before takeoff, but by the time our three-course meal arrived—including a hot fudge sundae and a steamy white towel—we had adjusted nicely.

Our jaws dropped, and our eyes bugged out when we walked into our suite at the five-star hotel in Santa Monica.

"We're not in Kansas anymore, Toto," I said, turning around and taking it all in—the enormous vase of fresh flowers from Nonfiction (the production company), the bowl of fruit and chocolates from Trisect (the agency), and the complimentary bottle of fine wine from the hotel.

"Holy cow!" I said, as John perused the room service menu. "Look at these plush white robes and slippers, hon! You don't get these at the Comfort Inn!"

"No," John said, "but you do get a free breakfast. Man, get a load of these prices!"

For the next few minutes, we ravaged the food basket like a couple of starving buzzards coming upon some fresh roadkill.

"Look at all this loot," my husband said. "Eat up! We'll never be able to squeeze this into our suitcases."

Not that our room was perfect, as John called to my attention. "Huh. There's no microwave, or refrigerator, or ironing board. And look at this," he said, opening the door to a cabinet where everything inside had a price written on it. "Can you believe this? Seven dollars for a little jar of M&Ms. Eight dollars for a handful of cashews! No, thank you! Here, hon, get a picture. Our friends won't believe this!" Then he shut the door firmly.

At the makeup trailer in Pasadena, I sat in the chair staring into a mirror surrounded by bright lights. When I apologized for my aging skin, Dina, who wore glittery bling in her blonde hair and called me "baby," reminded me that this was Hollywood, the land of illusion.

"You're beautiful!" she said. "And you are going to be even more beautiful! You should see your son. I did his makeup an hour ago."

When she finished, I stared into the mirror, hardly recognizing my transformed image. "Dina," I asked, "Have you ever considered moving to Baltimore? We have so many attractive features. . . ."

She thought I was kidding and laughed.

John was in Dina's makeup chair when Mike poked his head into the trailer. His makeup looked like mud that had been applied with a trowel. It was good to hear his reassuring words.

"They're gonna love you guys! Just be yourselves; pretend you're at home."

I wasn't sure that was the best advice to give John. I pictured him walking around the set in suspenders with a TV remote in his hand, a toothpick hanging from his mouth, and marveling at all those incredibly bright energy-consuming lights.

When our makeup was complete, Cindy escorted us up the street to the wardrobe trailer. Someone from production had contacted us weeks earlier for sizes and had me send our pictures. "What kind of clothes are you comfortable in?" they had asked. "What do you look good in, Mrs. Rowe?"

I was honest. "Well," I told the woman, "the more of my body we can cover up, the better I'll look. Long sleeves, long pants . . . Oh, and, my waistline disappeared sometime during the Clinton administration." We had laughed together, but I was happy to see several appropriate choices hanging in the trailer.

"Hey, these are nice," John said, looking down at his new shirt and jeans and shoes.

"They're yours," the nice wardrobe lady told him.

"Really? You mean to take home?" Things were definitely looking up.

When friends asked me what it was like to film a national commercial, I described a set filled with high-tech cameras and electronic sound equipment, the constant motion of sixty creative, high-energy professionals doing their job, a hand model for close-ups, two stand-ins, and the urge to giggle when a man clapped two boards together in front of my nose, saying, "Take nineteen! Quiet on the set!"

Most of all, I described a positive director the age of our granddaughters, who had all the qualities of a good teacher. A director who was encouraging, no matter how inept our performance. After each shot, she would say something like, "That was great! You guys are naturals! The cameras love you! Now this time when we do it, John, try not to deliver your line until Peggy stops talking. And Peggy, you don't need to remind John about stage directions; I'll take care of that. Just keep going until you hear the word *cut.*"

After we shot the first scene, Jason ran to the pharmacy to get John some decongestant and cough syrup—and insisted that there was no charge. "Really?" John said. These people were beyond generous.

Best of all was when our son appeared and gave us a thumbs-up. He was always close by with an encouraging word, but mostly, I remember the look of relief on his face after we had shot the first scene. Mike would later confess that he was as nervous as a mother duck crossing a busy intersection with her brood. He had, after all, promoted his parents over two professional actors—against the wishes of the client. Just as well he hadn't mentioned that to us.

We learned a lot about the making of commercials in those two days. First and foremost, there are three groups of people who must be satisfied before those magic words *Cut! It's a wrap!* are uttered: the client (in this case, Kimberly-Clark), the agency, and the production company. They were out of sight—all gathered before various monitors on the premises—watching the action. Some were in a large tent in the backyard during the filming and weighed in after each take. We soon learned to listen for those magic, welcome words, which were usually followed by cheers. The days were long, with a sumptuous, catered, sit-down meal at lunchtime, and snacks throughout the day.

At the end of the shoot on the second day, Mike, John, and I were treated like celebrities indeed when we entered the set—and received a standing ovation from the crew.

The following day, there was time for a little adventure, so Mike took us for a walk along Rodeo Drive, where the prices in the windows elevated John's heart rate to the equivalent of a three-mile run. At one point, he jumped backward in surprise and said, "Did you see that? $400 for a pair of jeans—with holes in the knees!" In doing so, he nearly knocked over a young pedestrian and apologized.

"Dad," Mike said, "Do you know who you just bumped into?" We looked at the girl who had moved on down the street—a little bit of a thing with long, stringy blonde hair.

"No. Should I?" John asked.

"That was Paris Hilton," Mike said.

"Never heard of her," he said, still recovering from sticker shock. He recuperated during our lunch al fresco at McCormick & Schmick's, where we had yet another adventure.

"Isn't it nice that you can go places without being recognized?" I said to our son as the waiter came over and handed us our menus.

"Don't you believe it. See all those phones? They're taking pictures. Try to look pleasant," he said, laughing.

While we were reading, a woman at a nearby table exclaimed loudly when a bird dropped a rather impressive calling card that splatted onto her menu and plate. When the waiter rushed over to clear away the mess, the woman's husband said, "Oh no, don't bother!" Then he stood up and pointed at Mike saying, "That guy over there will clean it up!" Naturally, we joined the people around us who were laughing. Some even applauded.

―――❖―――

Our first two Viva commercials were filmed on location in large rented houses in Pasadena and the San Fernando Valley. Our third Viva shoot, though, was by far the most exciting and was filmed on a Hollywood soundstage—where age spots, wrinkles, creaky joints, and figure flaws simply do not exist. The action was shot at the Hollywood Center Studios, Stage 9—famous for the filming of such shows as *I Love Lucy, Jeopardy, The Cosby Show,* and the movie *When Harry Met Sally.* To work on the same stage where Lucille Ball stood—on an assembly line at a conveyor belt stuffing candies into her mouth—was to walk on hallowed ground.

There were fewer surprises this time. I knew, for example, that the soundman would be clipping a battery pack to the waistband at the back of my slacks, and then dropping a mic down the front of my blouse. Afterward, he usually said something humorous like, "Okay, Mrs. Rowe, now you're ready to talk smack."

I wasn't shocked when Dina, wearing her makeup tool belt, rushed onto the set between takes (like AAA roadside assistance to change a flat tire during rush hour) saying, "Let me touch you up, baby," or when Nancy, the wardrobe mistress, stepped in to adjust my watch or my collar, then taped my blouse to my chest. Once, she even sewed a few stitches in my sleeves to keep them in place. I've always suspected that she switched size labels in the khakis to give me the illusion of fitting into a size 10 in Hollywood, (when I can barely squeeze into a size 12 in Baltimore).

Best of all, there was that same atmosphere of patience and respect for two senior would-be actors joining their son for the adventure of a lifetime. At the end of the first day when Mike and the crew invited us to join them in celebrating, my husband and I graciously declined, heading back to our hotel, instead, where we enjoyed our basket of goodies, a Jacuzzi, and a comfortable bed.

More than once I have marveled at the stamina and spirit of Betty White.

Has Hollywood changed our lives? To the extent that I've become more conscious of my appearance in public, perhaps. My comfortable old sweatpants and baggy sweatshirts are confined to our condo now.

When the Viva commercials were running, I felt like quite the celebrity. It wasn't unusual for friends, neighbors, and even strangers to approach me with a roll of Viva towels and ask for my autograph. So I made it a point to tell them that the claims made in the commercials were true. "Viva paper towels are absorbent and tough!" I'd say. When we went to parties, I always had the perfect hostess gift. Who doesn't love a free roll of paper towels—autographed?

I learned a lot on those shoots. Acting in commercials when your hands are disfigured with arthritis or when your figure isn't 36-26-36 is no deterrent. There are hand models for close-up shots. And body doubles for those long, tedious shots standing in the hot sun on location.

Our foray into the world of show biz was awesome, even if John and I did have to get down on our knees to clean up a "would be" tough mess in an oven. The good news was that our slender and younger stand-ins did the brunt of the kneeling and were the ones whose backsides were filmed.

I'll always remember the day I came face to face with a shocking reality. I had walked backstage after the shoot to hear my body double say to a small group, "I've been a hand double and a body double before, but this is the first time in my career I've ever been a *butt double!*" Everybody laughed while I backed away discreetly.

It was a revelation I could have done without!

⤖ FAMILY CELEBS ⤝

*I*T WAS A SATURDAY IN JULY, AND MIKE WAS IN town shooting a segment for *Dirty Jobs*. He had arranged to take the family to a local marina restaurant to celebrate his brother's birthday, and we were excited. Especially Katie and Jessie, who rarely saw their Uncle Mike since his move to California.

A warm afternoon breeze greeted us on the marina porch where a dozen or so other families were enjoying live music and Baltimore's finest steamed blue crabs right from the Chesapeake Bay. Our family of eight was shown to a table with a view of sailboats and powerboats gliding along the glassy river, some of them towing water skiers. We were settled and enjoying appetizers when a young man suddenly bolted from his boat and onto the pier shouting, "Hey, is that you, Mike Rowe? I could use some help cleaning out my bilge, man!"

Mike looked up from his appetizer, nodded, and waved. "I hear you, buddy," he said, as we all laughed.

An hour later when we'd finished our coffee and dessert, a dozen or so fans—mostly parents and children—had formed a line a respectful distance from Mike's chair. Our eleven- and fifteen-year-old granddaughters watched and shook their heads that people would find their Uncle Mike so interesting as to ask for an autograph and a picture. Go figure!

They were about to be even more amazed.

Mike signed the last autograph and posed for the final picture. As we all rose to leave, a man rushed from the restaurant onto the porch, as though escaping from a fire.

"Oh, Mike Rowe!" he begged. "My brother and his wife are having their wedding reception inside. They are your biggest fans, and it would make the day special for them if you'd stop in and say hello! Do you have a minute?"

Katie's jaw dropped, and she looked at her mother as if to say, "What kind of a bride needs an appearance from Uncle Mike in order to make her wedding day special? That's pitiful!"

Naturally he consented and followed the man inside. John and I weren't surprised. When your son makes a living before the public, you grow accustomed to fans showing their appreciation for his work. Just the day before, Mike had accompanied me to the grocery store across the street. We had barely gotten inside when, out of the blue, an elderly little man approached him, set a gallon of milk on the floor, and hugged him around the waist.

"Mike Rowe, do you know how proud we are of you? Yes sir! Every time I see you on TV, I say, 'Mike Rowe, you are doing your old neighborhood proud!' " It was so sweet, I found myself tearing up.

That evening we attended an Orioles game at Camden Yards. By the end of the second inning, complimentary glasses of beer lined the floor in front of our seats. Baltimoreans have a long memory. Before going national, our son had hosted a long-running local real estate show.

It wasn't always that way. There was a time when my husband and I were baffled by our son's celebrity. You see, John and I belong to a rare breed. We've never been movie goers, and we watch little TV. We have *never* asked anyone for an autograph—though I was allowed to hug a Budweiser Clydesdale once, which was better by far than an autograph.

Perhaps if I had been born a Redgrave or a Barrymore, Mike's celebrity would have seemed more natural to me. But I was a Knobel. Growing up, the closest my family ever came to celebrity was the night my mother pantomimed and lip-synced *I Didn't Know the Gun Was Loaded* onstage at the Overlea Lions Club variety show. It was pure torture for a fifteen-year-old daughter. My father, an electrician, was in charge of the lighting that evening.

As my mother sashayed seductively across the stage in my old cowgirl outfit, the long fringe swayed this way and that. She was Annie Oakley in heat, and I slid so low in my chair I was practically on the floor. I could only imagine how my poor father felt as he operated the spotlight that followed her around the stage. I wondered later if he'd been tempted to turn it off. I was grateful that my grandmother didn't have to witness this tasteless display by her oldest daughter.

When she brandished two loaded cap pistols and shot the man who had done her wrong, a boy sitting behind me whistled and said, "Hey, she's kind of sexy." I was still in shock when she lifted her leg and rested *my* cowboy boot on her victim's lifeless body. When she blew smoke from the barrel of her cap pistol, I actually got the dry heaves.

The audience didn't agree with me, obviously, as there was a standing ovation after the performance, and a man ran onto the stage with a big bouquet of flowers.

After the show, my parents invited me to the party in the banquet room of the Overlea Diner, but I declined. I was still feeling nauseous and asked to be dropped off at home. And here's the really bizarre part: in the car, Mom was all giggly and flirty, like it was opening night on Broadway or something, while Dad behaved as though he was sitting next to Marilyn Monroe. It was hard to watch, I can tell you that, and I couldn't wait to get in the house where I plopped Mom's flowers in a vase of water and took a spoonful of my father's antacid.

The next day at home, my mother carried those same flowers from room to room as she did her housework, humming *I Didn't Know the Gun Was Loaded* and looking all dreamy-eyed like she was getting a standing ovation all over again. She actually received congratulatory cards in the mail and displayed them on the refrigerator where she used to tape our report cards from school. She eventually came back down to earth—when the flowers wilted and petals littered the floor like a church aisle after a wedding.

My father's response to his own celebrity was quite the opposite on the Sundays he filled in for the preacher. When the adoring congregation praised his sermons and treated him like Billy Graham, he blushed with humility and assured them that any number of others in our church could have done just as well. My mother sat on the front pew on those Sundays, swinging her foot back and forth just like she had when she came to our school programs and we had a speaking part.

———◆———

Thanks to community theater, my husband had his own brush with celebrity. A faithful following of friends and family were strong supporters of John's plays—whether he was performing in a church or a college or an actual theater.

The cheers were so loud during curtain calls, John claimed to be embarrassed, (but between you and me, he smiled long after the applause ended).

One group of friends showed up at dinner theaters with a large sign that read John Rowe Fan Club. It was displayed in the middle of their table, which was always near the stage. Sometimes the spotlight fell on that sign, and it was like seeing my husband's name on a Broadway marquee. I was practically married to a real celebrity.

Our two younger sons reacted quite differently to their fifteen minutes of childhood celebrity. The youngest, Phil, was ten years old when he displayed his extensive rock and mineral collection at the local library. It was a pretty amazing assortment, most of which he had gathered from the stream in our neighborhood and during our family trips.

Phil was never an enthusiastic student, and I was desperate to get him involved in some activity that would encourage reading. Collecting rocks was the perfect hobby. He and I joined a rock and mineral club and before long were frequenting exhibitions and shows. Our basement and workshop were filled with boxes of rocks, and Phil was occupied researching rocks and minerals in library books—with help, of course.

An elderly member of our church was so impressed with our son's initiative that she gave him her own collection of minerals and gemstones. At the library, Phil's rocks were displayed in three categories: Igneous, Sedimentary, and Metamorphic, with a special classification for gems and minerals—all neatly labeled.

Our son took the positive recognition in stride. That is until his picture appeared in the local newspaper and people began calling. At that point, our resident celebrity talked about quitting school and becoming a full-time collector. His interest in rocks eventually waned, and he was content in the shadows until he reached high school and received much craved attention for his performances in an array of theatrical productions.

When our reserved middle son achieved the highest SAT scores in his high school, he kept it secret—until his brother heard the announcement over the school intercom. Scott's face turned red when the school applauded him. He discouraged us from talking about it. The following summer Scott was a hero and local celebrity for saving a drowning man's life at the pool where he was a lifeguard. At dinner that evening when I asked the children about their day, Scott casually mentioned that he might have saved a man's life at the pool. We pressed him for details.

"The pool was crowded when I noticed a man lying face down on the bottom at the deep end. I just jumped in and pulled him to the surface." He made it sound like business as usual, but we knew better.

"Wait a minute," we asked, forgetting about the food on our plates. "How did you get him off the bottom? How did you get him out of the pool? Was he unconscious? What did you do?"

"Well, he was about fifteen years old and easy to pull up. I put his arms over the side of the pool and crossed them, jumped out, and pulled him onto the pool deck. Then I rolled him onto his stomach, and he did the rest by himself. He threw up a gallon or so of water."

The knowledge that a mother could have lost her son that day had it not been for *my* son, was overwhelming. Scott admitted later that the incident had made him an instant celebrity at the Middle River pool, where kids said things like, "Gee Mr. Scott, you saved Larry's life! You're a hero, Mr. Scott!"

Years later, Mike introduced Scott, as well as his father and me, to an audience of thousands after he had just received the Distinguished Eagle Scout Award. In his acceptance speech, Mike held up the medal hanging around his neck and looked at Scott.

"See this, little brother? I'm distinguished." Everyone laughed, then Mike said, "My brother, Scott, doesn't have one of these. He doesn't have a *medal*. But my brother Scott has *mettle*. You see, some years ago, he jumped into deep water and saved a young man's life."

With that, there was a standing ovation for a reluctant hero and celebrity. John and I were proud—not just because Scott hadn't crawled beneath the table, but because he had saved a life.

———◆———

Our oldest son's childhood brush with celebrity came in middle school when he was honored as Most Outstanding Chorus Member before the entire student body. I had to learn about it on the streets, of course, and when I confronted him, he admitted that having his mother at the afternoon awards assembly would have made him nervous. His approach to Little League games was much the same, which I could never understand because he was a decent player.

"Please don't come," he used to beg us. "I don't like it when you watch me play; I do better when you're not there."

Now, I've heard stories about high-pressure parents who have unreasonable expectations for their kids—parents who verbally abuse coaches, referees, and umpires from the sidelines. I've personally witnessed red-faced fathers and mothers berating their own children from the bleachers for not performing up to their standards. I even read an article about a father who physically attacked a coach.

Our reward for being unobtrusive and cheering quietly was to be *un*invited to games. This meant dropping off our son at the ball field, parking a block away, then sneaking back and peeking through the bleachers like a couple of celebrity stalkers.

When *Dirty Jobs* soared to the top of the Discovery Channel's charts and Mike became a celebrity of sorts, I was confronted with a new identity: the dirty mother. People took my picture and asked me to autograph programs and menus. Neighbors I barely knew called out to me on my daily walks around the community.

"Hey, Mrs. Rowe, I saw your son in the San Francisco dump again last night. Ask him if he'd like to clean out our trash corrals on his next visit."

"Next time your son's here, Mrs. Rowe, tell him the storm drain in front of 9600 is clogged."

Another woman was curious about our celebrity's laundry. "Hey, Mrs. Rowe, does Mike bring those dirty clothes home when he visits?" she asked. "Are they gross?" I could tell she wanted all the "dirt," so I told her, "He just opens his suitcase, and his clothes march to the laundry room under their own steam." It's what she wanted to hear.

———◆◆◆———

My first unexpected moment of celebrity took place at the prestigious Kennedy Center in Washington, D.C., where John and I were guests during Mike's appearance with the National Symphony Orchestra. Leonard Slatkin, the music director, was a fan and invited our son to narrate a new orchestral work during a Saturday family concert.

Afterwards, Mike wandered through the various sections of the orchestra looking for "dirt." In the brass section, a trumpet player emptied his spit valve onto Mike's shoes. In the string section, a violinist explained that his bow was made of the finest hairs from the underneath side of a horse's tail—the hairs that touched the horse's *body.* The kids in the audience learned along with Mike that animal skins were used for drums, and the bones of dead animals were used to make the earliest woodwind instruments.

A year earlier, an episode of *Dirty Jobs* had been filmed in South Carolina, where a shrimp boat captain had taunted my son as he teetered precariously on the boom of the sailboat high above the water. Holding on for dear life as he swung through the air, Mike threatened, "When my mom sees this, she's gonna come down here and kick your pirate ass!"

Thanks to *Dirty Jobs* reruns, I experienced my own fifteen minutes of fame right there at the Kennedy Center. Mike had finished his trip through the sections of the orchestra and had just introduced us in the audience when a total stranger yelled to me over a dozen rows of seats.

"Hey, Mrs. Rowe! Have you kicked that pirate's ass yet?"

As I said, celebrity is *baffling*!

⇢ SOMETHING TO CHEW ON ⇠

Michael,

I called you last weekend. If your mailbox hadn't been full, I'd have told you something that would have knocked your socks off. Words I thought I would never utter.

Your father is having an affair...at Costco!

I know, you're thinking, Mom, get real! Don't laugh. I first became suspicious a few weeks ago when he came home late for dinner and smelling of truffles. Since then, I've been putting two and two together and, well, just listen to this and see what conclusion you come to.

Dad goes to Costco every Tuesday after Meals on Wheels while I play Mahjongg. "I go for the gas," he used to tell me, but now he comes home with a car full of stuff. And here's the kicker. Your father hates to shop! You know that! At Safeway and the mall, he waits for me in the car with his Kindle. That's why he has never been a gift giver; he doesn't like stores.

But now he frequents Costco with the urgency of your grandmother heading to Thursday night bingo at the home. He wouldn't think of skipping a Tuesday.

"That place is terrific, hon!" he'll say when he comes home. "They have everything!"

You have to pay membership dues and join Costco like it's a country club. Well, a country club without a golf course—or a golf pro or a swimming pool!

Last month, Dad came home with ten pounds of shelled pistachios and a gross of paper towels because, "A nice woman at Costco recommended them." He also came home with a bag of free hearing aid batteries from Kathy, the nice hearing specialist. Free, I tell you!

Once, when I questioned the wisdom of an eighty-five-year-old buying five gallons of V-8 juice, he shrugged and said, "It's okay. The woman at Costco says it has a long shelf life." And who is this woman who always seems to be around? Even when he calls to ask my advice on something that's on sale, I hear a woman's laughter in the background.

Now I'm not stupid, Mike, but my suspicions deepened recently when your father's hearty appetite began to wane—especially on Tuesdays. I found myself wondering if he was lovesick.

I should have been suspicious the day he came home and handed me a bag. "Here's a little present for you," he told me. Now that might not seem unusual, but as I've said, and as I'm sure you remember, your father is not a shopper. Intrigued, I peeked into the bag and saw what appeared to be aluminum. Hmm...Maybe one of those long, fold-up sun shields for the car window, I thought. Now that would be something Dad would give me.

I was wrong. It was a long, shiny, metallic-looking coat. Yeah! A coat! I put it on and was relieved to see that it was a size too small. I pulled it together in the front and stood before your father, feeling like a jumbo-sized roll of heavy-duty aluminum foil. Before I could say, "Thanks, hon, but doggone it, it's too small!" your father put his head back and laughed!

"Geez, Peg, if you had a funnel on your head, you'd look like Tin Man in The Wizard of Oz." And then he shook his head and said something very telling. "It looked different on the Costco lady."

As I said, I would have told you all this if you'd been home over the weekend. Anyway, I was feeling like a casualty of warehouse shopping, so this week I decided to skip Mahjongg and tag along to Costco with Dad to see for myself. And it's a good thing I did.

At the entrance, Cindy greeted your father by name and waved us in without even asking to see his card! Hmm…

After splitting a barbecue beef sandwich with extra slaw, we grabbed a shopping cart the size of our little red Scion xB and headed down the wide, crowded aisle.

"Good thing you brought your sweatshirt, hon," he said, pointing to the far end of the store. "No telling what the weather's like up in the outback." I usually laugh at his jokes, but I wasn't in the mood.

He played it cool, I can tell you that. And he was honest about coming for the gas. It sounded like a tuba was accompanying us through the store.

Suddenly, Dad made a sharp left. "Hey, Sheila, what do we have today, hon?"

The sample lady offered him a flirtatious smile, along with a Frisbee-sized waffle. Mine was the size of a communion wafer.

A minute later, after another tuba fanfare, Brenda shouted, "Hey, handsome, you're late! Come on over here and try some Cape Cod chicken salad with cranberries and pecans!"

Doris served a delicious mushroom flatbread, and in the deli section was Gladys, with a boned turkey breast and carving knife. Both women said it was so nice to see Dad again and kept the samples coming. I needed a pen and paper to keep track of the suspects. I also needed a nap.

At the checkout, though, there was cause for relief. Your father paused to discuss football with Charlie, and at the exit, stopped to argue politics with Lenny. At which point I came to the conclusion that I was mistaken. Dad is not having an affair at Costco. He's having an affair with Costco!

On the way home, I cracked the window and decided dinner could wait until Wednesday.

Anyway, I guess it's for the best that I couldn't reach you over the weekend. I'd have worried you needlessly.

Have a good day!

Love,
Mom

ON FAMILIAR GROUND:
→ROMANCING THE GARBAGE←

*M*Y HUSBAND AND I WERE VISITING OUR SON
Mike in San Francisco when he suggested walking to the village for a late breakfast al fresco. We were enjoying pancakes and eggs at a sidewalk cafe as a large garbage truck came to a screeching halt at the traffic light in front of us. A man clinging to the back end of the truck yelled loudly. "Hey, is that Mike Rowe I see?" The driver leaned out of the window and called, "Hey, Mike, how's it going, buddy?"

With other diners looking on, Mike called out, "Hey, Johnny! Hey, Joe! How 'bout a pancake." The light changed and the workers went on their way laughing, while people at the tables around us smiled at the local celebrity.

Over breakfast, our son proceeded to reminisce about the day he had spent with the Department of Sanitation and Waste Management in San Francisco for his show, *Dirty Jobs*. While it might not have been ideal table talk, Mike can always make us laugh. John and I remembered the very episode.

It was a sickening scene of putrid garbage marching along the conveyer belt—with congealed fat, rotting vegetables, hunks of meat in various stages of decay . . . and our son, picking through it like a finicky diner at an all-you-can-eat buffet. Suddenly, the conveyor belt picked up speed, and an image of Lucille Ball in a puffy white hat stuffing candies into her mouth popped into my mind.

"Don't you dare put that in your mouth!" I yelled at the young man on the screen, as my husband laughed, and Mike fell further and further behind in his current dirty job.

I should have known that garbage would figure prominently in our son's career. Even now, when I watch *Dirty Jobs* reruns, I'm reminded that Mike's relationship with garbage goes way back. I can't help wondering if his father and I played a minor role in his career outcome.

Our son performed his earliest chore as a two- or three-year-old when he placed the family trash and garbage in the cans behind our house. While this might sound pretty routine, mundane even, as chores go, our little one was a bit of a neat freak. Neat freak as in: Every two minutes he waved his hands in the air and whined from his high chair, "Wash my geesy hands!" John likes to tell people they were his very first words, but that's not true. His first words were "icky" and "yucky."

Oh yeah, little Mike was a fuddy-duddy. From early on, he refused to touch anything messy—nasty substances such as Play-Doh and finger paint and food . . .

His father and I cheered him on from the doorway as his little hands reached up, carefully removed the lid from the garbage can, made the drop, and replaced the lid.

"Aw," I'd say. "He's such a responsible child!" John claimed he looked like he was making a bank deposit. Mike outgrew his neatness fetish, and as his younger brothers took over that mundane chore behind the house, our oldest moved up the ladder in the world of garbage. Every evening after dinner, in the spirit of Meals on Wheels, he delivered leftovers and table scraps to wildlife in the back field using his little red wagon. Turkey carcasses, ham fat, apple peelings . . . By morning, the deposits he made beneath the mulberry tree at the edge of the woods had vanished—like magic. Over time, we would watch all three of our sons make that daily trek to the back field pulling the wagon.

When Mike was eight, another milestone was marked in his relationship with refuse. That was the year he was entrusted with his grandparents' garbage as well as ours *and* the tractor.

He heaved the metal cans onto our tractor cart like the professionals who empty them onto the garbage trucks—and drove them down the 800-foot lane and across the bridge with such an air of importance, his grandfather observed with a chuckle, "You'd think he was hauling a shipment of gold for Wells Fargo."

―――――❖――――――

One of the perks of country living is that your kids get to practice driving the family station wagon around the field when they're only fourteen. With his father seated beside him, Mike bounced over the rough pasture, swerving around trees and horses and wooden jumps. Before long, just as he had graduated from the little red wagon to the tractor and cart, our oldest son moved on to transporting garbage and trash in the family car. On Thursday evenings, he helped his dad load heavy cans into the back of the station wagon, and together, with Mike at the helm, they delivered them to the end of the lane. He took his job seriously, and before long, John felt that he was ready to fly solo.

We could scarcely finish our dinner on Thursday evenings before the frenzied rush was on.

"Last call for garbage!" our son would announce, sounding like the announcer over the airport intercom. After gulping his dessert, Mike was a blur, snatching up our plates, scraping them into a bag, and spiriting it to the cans the way a Pony Express rider rushed the mail to his waiting horse. Instead of the jangle of spurs on boots, it was the jangle of car keys in his pocket.

"Be careful," I called behind him, as I had the week before, and the week before that—because that's what mothers do. There was little to worry about other than meeting one of the three neighbors who shared the single-lane, stone driveway—in which case there was plenty of room to pull off onto the grass.

"Yeah, Mike," his brother warned him. "No playing chicken with Mr. Willie tonight." The thought of our senior neighbor engaging in a game of chicken always brought laughter from the brothers. I knew that wasn't going to happen. Still, I always watched from the window until the family vehicle pulled back into the driveway minutes later.

One Thursday evening Mike returned with a sober look. On his way downstairs to finish his homework, he said quietly, "Dad, it felt like one of the front tires might need some air."

"Thanks, son," John said, reaching for the flashlight. His wink to me said: *Do you know how fortunate we are to have such a conscientious son?* Minutes later, he returned and called Mike up to the kitchen.

"You were right," John said calmly. "The left front tire is low on air." Then, leaning a few mere inches from Mike's face, he said, "That's what happens when a tire is knocked off the rim. Too much speed on the bridge, young man! You hit the beam on the side. Put on your old jeans."

Mike learned to change a tire that night—without complaining.

—⋙⋗◆⋘⋖—

The Thursday evening I drove fifteen-year-old Mike to a school friend's cookout a couple of miles away, I saw another side of the young man who had made a career of commandeering the family garbage. That evening he loaded the cans of garbage and trash into the back of the station wagon as usual, to be dropped off at the end of the lane on his way to the party. We were a block from his friend's house and could see the kids playing volleyball on the side lawn when Mike turned around and noticed the cans and various large items of trash flopping and twirling in the breeze as they protruded through the open tailgate.

We had forgotten to unload the garbage.

"Stop the car!" Mike yelled with an urgency that made me think I had run over a pedestrian. "You can just let me out here; I'll walk the rest of the way." God forbid his friends should see him get out of a vehicle with garbage and trash in it. He looked relieved to see me turn around in a driveway and head for home.

The night Mike was featured at the San Francisco dump surrounded by mountains of garbage, I reminded him of that fifteen-year-old boy who had been mortified at the thought of being seen with the family trash and garbage. "And look at you now," I said as we viewed the episode together. "Millions of people are watching you."

When his high school friends took jobs in restaurants after graduation, Mike said, "No thanks!" He'd had his fill of scraping plates, clearing tables, and emptying garbage. He couldn't believe his good fortune when he landed a job at the nearby Gunpowder Falls State Park.

"It's outside! And almost like being a park ranger," he told us.

At dinner after his first day on the job, we were all curious. Mike rolled his eyes.

"I rode around in the back of an open truck and picked up smelly garbage cans. Then I got to scrub them. Whoopee."

Unfortunately, our son would have more than just memories of the cruel irony of that first paying dirty job at the park.

It came late on a summer afternoon and was the kind of phone call parents dread.

"Hi Mom," Mike said, sounding casual. "Um . . . I had a little accident today, but I'm okay, so don't worry."

"What? Where are you?" I asked, trying unsuccessfully not to sound frantic. At the hospital where he waited for us in the emergency department, our son was barely recognizable behind swelling, stitches, bruising, and bandages.

It seems the irresponsible young driver of the open truck he was riding on had sped off, causing Mike to tumble off the back and onto the gravel road. The result of that prank was a broken nose, cuts, and scrapes to his hands and face.

There was but one certainty in Mike's mind at the end of that summer: there would be no room in his future for garbage.

I recalled that infamous summer job the night I watched Mike on *Dirty Jobs* dashing through the narrow alleyways of Chinatown with a sack of garbage slung over his shoulder, looking like a Santa Clause from a bad dream. Later, I uttered a silent prayer when he hung precariously to the outside of the vehicle as it negotiated the hilly streets of San Francisco.

Whether my son is driving a truck with liquid garbage sloshing onto him from above or operating a homemade contraption to deliver slop to the pigs on a farm, I'm sure of one thing: Mike Rowe is on familiar ground!

→ THE LONG RIDE HOME ←

Mike,

*T*hanks for everything. It was a great visit. We just got in the door at 6:30 a.m. The flight was fine, but I won't recover from the drive home anytime soon.

Just an hour ago a black SUV lurched to a stop at the curb outside the United terminal. The driver jumped out and held up a tablet that said ROWE.

I raised my hand. "That's us."

"She was supposed to meet us inside," Dad whispered. "Well don't say anything. She looks frazzled," I said.

The young woman wore a full-length wool coat in the chilly morning air. Her head scarf looked as though she'd walked through hurricane winds, and a long shock of dark hair covered half of her face. Every few seconds she threw her head back, stuck out her jaw, and blew the hair away from her face with a vengeance.

"Give me suitcases!" she barked. I thought she was joking. She sounded Russian, and she was on a mission. But she grabbed the smaller carry-on from me, and after several frantic, unsuccessful attempts to push in the retractable handle, she yanked the bag off the sidewalk and slung it into the trunk. I looked around wondering if airport security was bearing down on us, but they were nowhere in sight.

"Hey, wait a minute!" your father said, taking the carry-on from the trunk and gently pushing the handle in. "Be careful!" Before I could remind him that he has a hernia, he lifted the other two suitcases and carefully placed them into the trunk.

"You seen what they do to your suitcases?" the woman asked, nodding toward the terminal, then slamming the trunk lid and blowing the hair from her face.

"Well, I don't have to watch it!" Lack of sleep on the red eye from California was catching up with your father. It was going to be a long ride home, I could tell.

"This not my job," our driver said when we were on our way. "I do favor for company."

"Would you rather we call an Uber?" your sleep-deprived father asked. "Because we can do that."

The Italian dinner I'd scarfed down on the plane hours earlier was speaking to me, and I reached into my purse for a Tums.

"No, no! I say I do it, I do it! But can't be late for own customer—I pick up in Annapolis 7:30. Traffic bad."

"Do you know where we're going?" I asked.

"I have GPS."

We were barely away from the terminal when the car stopped short and jerked right into the next lane.

"Hey, what the...?" said Dad, getting off the floor.

"John, I told you to put your seatbelt on! Quick!"

"That car stop in middle of road, no reason!" she said as a small bottle hanging from the rearview mirror swung back and forth like a pendulum on steroids, making a ping, ping, ping sound.

"Well, no wonder! What in blazes is that thing stuck to the middle of your windshield?" Dad asked, pointing to something the size of a pan pizza. "It's blocking your vision!"

"It's GPS," she said.

"You should move it to the right, under the mirror," said Dad.

"That's what my husband say. I see okay." She gave a dismissive gesture with her right hand, smacking the bottle and sending it off again. Ping, ping, ping.

In the back seat, Dad looked at me over his glasses. "I wanted us to get an Uber, but you said, 'Oh, no, hon, let's reserve a car. They're luxurious and dependable—and they come into the airport for you and help with your luggage.'" He leaned a little closer. "Is this enough luxury for you?"

Minutes later, the driver screamed, "Oh no! This is toll road?!" In the rearview mirror, her dark eyes were as round as drink coasters.

"Yes," I said. "It takes us through the Harbor Tunnel."

She shook her head and threw her hands into the air. "The company no pay for toll. I pay on my E-ZPass! I make nothing! And now I'm late for own customer." Ping, ping, ping, ping.

Your father's seatbelt clicked, then he pointed to two packages of Fig Newtons and two bottles of water in the console between us— grinning as though he had discovered gold.

"They're probably for own customer," I whispered as Dad began removing a cellophane wrapper.

"We deserve these. Here! Take it! Eat it!" It was like being served communion by a priest who had a flight to catch. Within seconds, we were washing down the sweet cookies with bottled water.

My heart was still thumping when I heard your father say, "Turn left here," to which our driver responded with attitude, "I have GPS."

At last—we were home!

"It's only 6:30. You should be in Annapolis by 7:30," I told her.

"Here you are," Dad said, handing her a generous tip—which surprised me because our gratuities are always prepaid. I was even more surprised when she handed your father her business card— and he took it (without laughing).

As the black SUV tore out of the driveway and into the boulevard on two wheels, Dad looked at me and shrugged. "She's just trying to earn a living."

On the elevator, your father handed me the card and said, "You do realize that there is no way she's going to make Annapolis by 7:30."

Actually, I felt kind of sorry for her. That said, her card has mysteriously disappeared.

Love,
Mom

→ THE DOCTOR IS IN ←

Hi Mike,

*H*ave you found a doctor yet? You're over fifty and should be having regular check-ups—including a colonoscopy! Speaking of doctors, I want to tell you something about our general practitioner.

One evening after dinner your father read a long magazine article aloud to me from The New Yorker. It was about chronic fatigue syndrome, and the following morning I was too tired to even get out of bed. Dad thinks I'm overly susceptible to the power of suggestion. One thing for sure, there was no way I was going to tell my doctor. You've met Dr. Lisa—the GP who specializes in sarcasm and hypochondria. Instead of treating me like an intelligent, informed adult, she accuses me of self-diagnosing.

Remember the year I broke my left foot in Yosemite? Well, after it healed, I told her my left leg looked larger than my right leg. My exact words were, "I think I have lymphedema in my left leg. I've seen people in the nursing home with the condition and..."

"I don't see any signs of lymphedema," she said, looking at my leg and shaking her head.

"But when I'm in the shower and look down, my left leg definitely appears larger than my right one," I told her.

You know what her advice was? "Don't look down at your legs while you're in the shower."

Now, I ask you, your father thought she was kidding but I beg to differ. When we got back from visiting your brothers in Florida last winter, I wasn't feeling well and told Dr. Lisa I might have dengue fever.

"Margaret," she said in a voice you would use to speak to a child, (yeah, she calls me by my formal name). "You do not have a tropical disease." Of course, I didn't mention I had just finished a John Grisham novel where the main character suffered with the disease. "Well, I feel awful," I said. "Maybe you should just put me down."

Instead of encouraging me, she said, "That's a good idea. Sure, I can put you down." Then she leaned toward me and said, "Because putting people down is how I get my kicks!"

I still remember that day I noticed an itch behind my knee. It was a tiny black tick, so I pulled it off, wrapped it in a plastic baggie and hurried to Dr. Lisa's office.

"Look," I said. "This tick bit me behind the knee, and it hurts. I brought it along so you could do an autopsy. He might have Lyme disease."

She chuckled and rolled her eyes. Then, in a voice dripping with sarcasm, she said, "I don't do autopsies here in the office, Margaret, but let's take a look at that bite."

At least she took me seriously. Turns out there was a red bull's-eye, so she cleaned it up and prescribed the appropriate antibiotic. She actually complimented me on coming in promptly—so, of course, I passed out right there on the floor.

One time she laughed out loud at me. "Don't be silly, Margaret. Leprosy has been all but eradicated in the civilized world. That's osteoarthritis in your finger!"

Your father is a different story altogether. I have to force him to go to the doctor. When we both had the flu last winter, Dr. Lisa asked me how he was doing.

"Oh, he has a wicked cold," I told her. She shook her head and rolled her eyes. "God forbid he should come in and get something to make him feel better."

Anyway, Mike, wait until you hear the latest. My gynecologist of many years recently retired. Not to over dramatize, but it was an event of cataclysmic proportion—the equivalent of a 7.5 on the Richter scale. Dr. Pearson wasn't just any doctor. He was a cross between Marcus Welby and Mr. Rogers, and the neighborhood would not be the same without him. So, I asked Dr. Lisa if she'd like to recommend someone. She thought for a minute and wrote his name on a paper.

"So, what's he like?" I asked. "Is he any good?"

"No, Margaret, he's a butcher with no medical experience," she replied. See what I mean? The woman constantly acts like she has a bus to catch, but always has time for sarcasm!

"Well, he's a little different from Dr. Pearson. But he's experienced and people tell me they like him." I would discover later that she'd left out one small detail—and I think she did it on purpose.

I had my first appointment last week. The doctor's assistant put me in a gown and positioned me on the examining table, then left, saying, "Dr. Berenstain will be with you in a minute." I'm normally nervous in that situation anyway, but with a new doctor, I was practically hyperventilating.

A minute later, the door opened, then closed, but I saw no one from my supine position—though I thought I heard footsteps. Suddenly, from under the paper sheet, somewhere in the vicinity of my stocking feet, came an adult male voice.

"Hello, Mrs. Rowe. I'm going to ..." I popped up like a frozen waffle from the toaster and beheld a perfectly proportioned man the height of a barstool at the end of the examining table. He was not sitting. He was standing. My sudden movement must have unnerved him, as his eyes were as big and round as donut holes. The eyes were the only part of his face I saw before quickly looking away. I'm a great proponent of diversity and inclusion, and I wouldn't think of staring.

I once again assumed the position and remember nothing about the examination, except that it was conducted in absolute silence. I remembered some advice Dr. Marcus Welby had given to a young medical student: "You need to get closer to your work." Hmm ... I wondered if Dr. Berenstain had seen that episode. I was brought back to reality when he said, "I'll talk to you in my office, Mrs. Rowe." And he was gone.

Your father's comment was predictably practical: "Well, he probably had nice small hands." (Hope this isn't TMI.)

Anyway, Mike, I'm going to stick with Dr. Lisa. After all, she has kept me alive for the past twenty-seven years, and I'm beginning to think she might have a sense of humor after all. Actually, I've been meaning to make an appointment with her. My eyes have been bloodshot, I'm lethargic, I have a dry cough, and my nose is warm. I'm pretty sure it's distemper. Can't wait to tell her.

Love you, Mike. I'll let you know what she says. I doubt that it's hereditary.

Mom

P.S. Too bad you don't live closer. You could go to Dr. Lisa too. I have referred several people to her—even some that I like.

Dad's in recovery. Surgery went well. Repaired hydrocele and hernia, removed old mesh, put in new. Dr. says he can expect extreme swelling and bruising and difficulty urinating. Wants to give you a colonoscopy next time you're in town. Says it's a real dirty job. Do you think that's professional? I'll keep you posted. Love you. Mom

January 21, 2018

Mike, your father is in the bathroom reading his tablet and just yelled out at me to tell you something. A man in California passed a five-foot tapeworm that came from eating sushi. They think salmon. Anyway, he thought his intestines were coming out and he was dying. Dad knows how much you like sushi and says that you should not eat it anymore! I told him that when you have tapeworms, you lose a lot of weight. You're probably safe. We love you, Mike. Mom

⇢ THE OLD GRAY PAIR ⇠

"*I*N THE SPRING, A YOUNG MAN'S FANCY lightly turns to thoughts of love." Alfred Lord Tennyson was twenty-six when he made this observation. How typical of someone that age to think that spring ignites a fire only in the young.

⇒◆⇐

My husband called me to the window this morning after breakfast. "Look at this!" he said. Two sparrows locked in mortal combat were rolling around the balcony floor, crashing into the railing and stirring up dust.

"Oh no! Do something before they kill each other!"

"Look again," John said. "They're getting it on!"

At that point, the coupled birds lifted off as one and fluttered through the air.

"Well, it is spring," I reminded my husband, as he locked me in an embrace and whispered in my ear. "So, what do you say, babe? You have a half hour?"

Now, my beloved is an octogenarian, but I'm here to tell you that love is no less vibrant just because we've reached a certain age. It simply takes on a different hue.

"All right," I sighed, as he reached into his pants pocket and pulled out a deck of cards, sat down at the kitchen table, and proceeded to deal two hands. "But I can only play until noon. I have a busy day."

<hr />

Spring has always been my favorite season. A few years ago, we spent March in Florida. One morning as we were having coffee and reading the paper on our veranda, we watched as an older couple across the courtyard tottered onto their patio and sat facing each other. As the woman put her head back to enjoy the sun, her husband lifted her feet, and for the next hour, clipped her toenails, pausing from time to time to enjoy a drink and brush clippings from his thighs. When he finished, his wife trimmed the hairs in his ears and nose.

"Aw, how sweet is that?" I said, taking my husband's hand.

"Huh . . . Like a couple of primates in a grooming frenzy."

Some people are more sentimental than others. At that point, John backed up to the wall and scratched his itchy back. I was tempted to tell him how much he reminded me of my old horse who rubbed his itchy tail on the rough tree bark in the pasture, but why spoil the moment?

<hr />

I love my family albums with pictures of my mother and father when they were young and vital. Growing up, they seemed ancient. No child wants to see his parents as sexual creatures; old and cute and harmless is what they want. Holding hands is acceptable.

One evening after dinner, my husband and I were hugging in the kitchen when our visiting son wrapped his arms around us and lifted us off the floor saying, "You guys are adorable!" I wondered what he'd have said if he'd seen us at bedtime.

"Do you have the stuff?" John asked me as I got in bed.

"Of course," I said. "You do me first."

"Uh-uh. You know how you are; you get too steamy. You do me first."

"All right, but you'd better not fall asleep," I warned him. I love to hear his groans of ecstasy as I do my thing.

Nothing relieves my husband's itchy back like cortisone cream. And what he said about me is true. Ben Gay on my shoulders and neck can produce too much heat if he's not careful.

John knows what I like.

→ TIME TO COME CLEAN! ←

Hey, Mike,

You just said something so funny on an interview I listened to. Somebody asked you about your parents, and you told them we had moved into a condominium. That was true, of course, but then you said something that literally made me laugh out loud: "I was afraid they'd have a hard time leaving the home where they'd raised three children, but the transition was smooth, and they adjusted immediately to condo life. They fit right in."

Obviously, I don't tell you and your brothers everything, Mike. Maybe it's time I came clean.

It's no secret that I am sometimes a dreamer. When your dad and I were approaching our seventies, I would dream about your father putting his arms around me and saying, "You and I are getting a little long in the tooth, hon. Maybe it's time we moved into one of those condominiums and turned this place over to some younger folk. Whaddaya say?"

Oh yeah, I was a dreamer all right. I still remember your father's real reaction when I first broached the subject of moving.

"What do you mean they'll cut the grass and shovel the snow for us? What am I, decrepit? I have a perfectly good tractor and snow shovel. It'll be a cold day in 'you know where' when I go to live in a con-do-min-i-um!"

At least I had planted the seed, I told myself as Dad continued climbing up trees with a 10-pound Stihl chain saw strapped to his waist…or onto the roof to clean out clogged rain gutters…or into a hole to clean out the septic tank. I had to admit that his pioneer spirit was admirable. He had spunk and had been my hero more times than I could remember.

Like the Saturday morning I found a snake in the basement laundry room and screamed. Dad trapped it, grabbed him behind the head, and released him in the field. He pretty much did the same thing when a mouse found its way into our bathroom while I was showering. Dad calmly reached down, picked him up by the tail, and headed for the back door. Then there was the big hairy spider in the bed and the sparrow that fluttered down the chimney flu, both of which your father dispatched handily. Later, when I bragged about him to my friends, he said, "You might want to think twice about that. It could be seen as a commentary on your housekeeping."

So I waited patiently for him to be ready for the move to a condo. And then one afternoon I came home and found a bloody baseball cap in the bathroom sink—and no sign of your father.

I eventually found him—in the emergency room of Franklin Square Medical Center getting sutures in his scalp. He'd been cutting down a dead tree in the woods when a branch broke off and landed on his head. I'm afraid I wasn't very sympathetic.

"Who do you think you are, John? Daniel Boone? We should be seeing the world, like the Hubers! At this very moment, they're on a bus tour in New England. All they had to do was shut off the water and lock their condominium door. As simple as that. And look at you—splitting logs, shoveling ashes from a wood stove, and now, hanging out in the ER."

Your pioneer father was in stubborn denial, of course, but every once in a while, out of the blue, he would say something that gave me a glimmer of hope. Like, "Do you really want to live in a building with thirty strangers, Peg?" Or, "Women are supposed to be sentimental. Have you forgotten you raised three children in this house?"

Then came "the week from hell." The septic tank overflowed, the water pump burned up, and the tractor stopped running. And, no, it wasn't my doing! (Like I would even know how.)

Looking back, convincing your father was the easy part. The real nightmare didn't begin until the day after we moved into our lovely condominium, and Dad headed to the balcony with our dinner scraps.

"Where are you going with that garbage?" I asked.

"I'm going to throw it to the animals."

You might remember that our routine at home was to carry garbage to the back field where nature's "disposals" performed their Houdini magic and leftovers disappeared before morning.

"Look, hon!" I said, running to the sink and turning on the garbage disposal. His eyes narrowed at the thought of perfectly good garbage going to waste.

"John, there are no wild animals in this community, and throwing garbage from the balcony is against the condo rules!"

Later, I thought it wise to choose my battles carefully and look the other way when he left for his evening strolls, pockets bulging with stale biscuits and other contraband. At least it's dark, I'd tell myself. And the neighbors won't report him to the board.

The worst was laundry day. After retiring, Dad took on some of my domestic chores. I'm sure I told you.

"It's only fair," he'd say. "After all, you're still teaching part-time."

At no other time had his compulsive organizing been more evident than under our backyard clotheslines—where a long row of socks hung in pairs, side by side, heels facing west. Underpants were strung together like a train of freight cars, and, on the back lines, towels and sheets were suspended in color-coded symmetry.

"It's important to have a system," he'd tell me, as though I had simply slung the wash toward the clotheslines for the past thirty years and hoped for the best.

He was putting the clothes from our condo washing machine into the laundry basket when he asked, "Hon, where is the community clothesline, anyway? I don't remember seeing it."

"Well," I said, steadying my thumping heart with one hand and patting the dryer with the other. "This is it."

I could have gone with sarcasm and said, "It's out there beside the community spa, and dance hall, and putting green." But your father's a very literal person. I didn't want to give him false hope.

His jaw dropped, and he stared blankly, as though I had just told him George Jetson would hook our laundry to the back of his space car and circle the earth until it was dry.

I smiled cheerfully. "No more standing in the hot sun or cold wind." Then I swung open the dryer door and gave my best pitch.

"Twenty-five minutes and, voilà!"

"Are you out of your mind?" he asked, heading for the balcony door. "I'll hang them over the railing before I put them in that energy hog!"

"It's against the condo rules!" I shouted.

I'm afraid life was a downward spiral after that.

"What do you mean I can't take a walk in my undershirt?"

"What do you mean I can't go down to the lobby for the paper in my pajamas?"

"What do you mean I can't shake this rug? Why do we even have a balcony?"

"What do you mean I can't wash my car?" Bless his heart. I wanted to hug him as he stood there with his little bucket of rags and sponges and special soap, looking like a kid who has been told there's no Santa Claus.

And so it went....

That was the real beginning of Dad's life in the shadows. Now, before bedtime, he turns off the kitchen lights and (in his pajamas), slips onto the balcony like a cat burglar making off with a tablecloth or a scatter rug. There, he defiles the "common area" below with crumbs and dust, while I keep a lookout for dog walkers and headlights.

"Voilà!" he'll say, looking at me and closing the kitchen door triumphantly. I don't appreciate it when he refers to us as Bonnie and Clyde. I prefer my new nickname for him: The Prince of Darkness.

Christmas will be here before long, and Dad has been eyeing a red Santa Claus with flashing red and green lights for the balcony. Sooner or later I'm going to have to tell him about the "white lights only" rule for the outside. Sigh....

And now, it seems, your father has made an enemy in our building. It happened one afternoon in August when we propped our hallway door open while we carried some packages in. Suddenly I looked up to see a neighbor standing in the doorway with his arms crossed like Mr. Clean—minus the smile.

Our neighbor Ed is the self-appointed condo police, roaming the neighborhood in search of dog walkers who don't pick up, people who don't break down their cardboard boxes before putting them in the trash corral, and neighbors who throw food out for the birds after dark. Neighbors pretty much ignore him as he roams our building checking the temperature in the common area and searching for rule infractions.

"You can't leave this door open!" he announced.

Now, when it comes to getting along peacefully, Dad and I are like Quakers.

"Come on in, Ed, and have a seat," I said, as Dad was in the other room. "You've never visited us before."

"You can't leave this door open!" he repeated, a little louder. "You're sucking up all the cold air from the common area! Close it now!"

I guess everybody has a breaking point, even Quakers, and for your father, this was it. Suddenly, a great whoosh of wind came from behind me like one of those tornado funnel clouds, brushing against my left side, practically spinning me around. Next thing I knew, The Prince of Darkness was standing in the doorway toe-to-toe with Mr. Clean—still minus the smile.

"I'll close this door when I'm good and ready! And not before!" Then, with his hands on his hips, Prince leaned closer and looked up at our neighbor. "That cold air is just as much mine as it is yours, and I'll suck it up as much as I please!"

Honestly, Mike, scary as it was, I have to say I was proud of your father and was reminded of his treatment of the snake in the basement, and that mouse on the bathroom floor, and the spider in the bed. Like Albert Schweitzer, he had always released his prey, and I hoped Ed would fare as well.

"Oh, yeah?" Ed said, his shoulders drooping. "Well ... well ... I'm going to report you to the board!" He sounded like a second grader threatening to report a bully to the safety patrol.

"Go ahead! See if I care!" said Dad. I might have laughed—if I hadn't been worried about bloodstains on our new foyer rug.

Ed left, and we kept the hall door open the rest of the day—just because. So much for privacy.

The following day on my walk around the community, I came upon a small gathering of neighbors I recognized as board members. After greeting one another, one of the men said to me, with exaggerated anger, "Mrs. Rowe, are you and your husband still sucking up that cold air from the common area?" We all had a good laugh, and that was that.

Ed's a lot more mellow these days, but I still hold my breath when Prince sneaks onto the balcony after dark.

Love you,
Mom

⇥ AFTERNOON DELIGHT ⇤

J WAS SITTING AT MY COMPUTER BY THE window when I looked up and saw the little red car zip into our parking space and an old man jump out.

"Oh, no," I thought, glancing at the clock. "Three thirty p.m. My heart can't take this excitement."

I unlocked the door, and a second later my husband appeared, hugged me tightly, then backed up and said, "Whaddaya think? You wanna?"

"Oh, John, really, we're getting too old for this. It's too much pressure, and we don't have enough time."

"Sure, we do," he said, looking at his watch, then giving me a come-hither stare.

I headed for the bedroom with Peter Pan on my heels. He tore off his hospital volunteer shirt and hurried to the bathroom while I removed my blouse and stepped into the closet. John was leaving the bathroom when I came from the closet and threw him a shirt. I put on a presentable blouse, then scurried into the bathroom for lipstick and a quick comb through.

"Come on, you don't need to do that. You look great," he said, tucking in his shirt. (My husband always says that.) He handed me "Old Blue," and we rushed down the steps and got into "Red Rocket," John's affectionate name for his late-life-crisis toy.

I have to admit that behind the wheel of the cherry red Scion xB, wearing his bright blue shirt, John looked like a young man—not a gentleman of eighty-five with whistling hearing aids, a squeaky foot brace, and a groaning hernia. I held onto the handle above the door as we zoomed onto the boulevard and headed south.

At a red light, we looked frantically at the clock on the dashboard. "Gonna be close!" my husband said. He has always been a thrill seeker. Me? I closed my eyes. Minutes later, we pulled into a parking spot at our destination with only seconds to spare.

John usually opens my door, but there was no time for such niceties today. We hopped from the car as though we were afraid of missing the overture at a hot-ticket Broadway musical, and ran through the door, stepping behind the last person in line just before the man pulled the rope across the aisle behind us and snapped it to the pole.

Phew! Anybody who thinks that true adventure and excitement are behind you when you've reached your eighties, clearly hasn't experienced the Early Bird Senior Buffet Special at the Golden Corral.

Be warned: prices go up at 4 o'clock.

→ THE AUTO TRAIN ←

Michael,

*I*n case you're wondering, your father and I have returned safely from our visit with family—and are still alive. Your brothers, sister-in-law, and nieces send their love. (I'm including photos in case you don't remember them.)

Perhaps I've mentioned that your father and I took the Auto Train to and from Florida this year—a first for us. It was Dad's idea, and I'm afraid I wasn't too receptive in the beginning.

"It sounds like some modern-day version of Murder on the Orient Express," I said.

"Don't be silly," your father said. "No stranger is going to murder us on a train. You watch too much PBS. If you let Agatha Christie rule your life, you'll never leave the house."

Well, after spending a total of thirty-four hours aboard the Auto Train with your father, I'm here to say that he's absolutely right. No stranger is going to murder you. It will more likely be your traveling companion—the person who's glued to you like a shadow and sharing your roomette.

Dad says it's called a roomette because it looks like somebody "ette" your "room," leaving you in a phone booth with two options: sit or stand. Of course, you could always slide the door open and jump into the aisle, which is what we did while an attendant transformed our two chairs into my bed, then released Dad's upper bunk from the ceiling.

At bedtime, your father was climbing the walls, literally. Instead of putting his left foot on my face, he opted to place it on a tiny shelf on the wall and throw his right leg over the edge of the bed like he was mounting a Budweiser Clydesdale. Once in place, he wrapped some straps around his rear end and hooked them to the ceiling so he wouldn't roll off the bed, through the door, and down the aisle in the middle of the night. Honestly, Mike, it looked like he was strapped in a space capsule ready for liftoff. Either that or he was in some kind of porn movie. Not that I've ever seen one....

Thanks to his eighty-six-year-old prostate, Dad had to dismount twice during the night and zigzag thirty feet down the aisle to the toilet. He should have counted his blessings. At least he could approach it straight on and take care of business like a man. When it was my turn, I had to open the restroom door from the aisle, adjust my clothing, turn around, and back up to the toilet. (I know, TMI.)

All I can say is, I was pretty smart to monitor my liquid intake at dinner.

We survived the trip south and upgraded to something called the Bedroom on the trip home. What an improvement! We had a whole extra square foot of space. It was like being on the open prairie. We could actually turn around (one at a time). And we had a private bathroom. They call it that because, if you lower the toilet lid, sit down with your nose five inches from the door, and turn a little knob on the wall, you're sprinkled with water from above—like the way produce is sprinkled at the Giant Food Store.

The real perk in the Bedroom is the basin, where, if you sit on the lower bunk, you can lean over and wash your hands or brush your teeth. The faucet vibrates and sounds like a bull elephant during mating season. (I know this because when I'm not watching *Dirty*

Jobs, I'm watching the Nature channel.)

I hope I don't sound like a complainer, Mike. You know I'm a positive person. And like your father says, "Hey, the Auto Train beats driving 1,710 miles on I-95!"

The dining car was fun. Good food, congenial companions, and great service. After an hour, I thought your father was going to adopt our waiter. We know where he lives, all about his family, and his work history. The following morning at breakfast, he greeted Dad like a favorite uncle. Later, when we got into our car, I looked back to make sure the young man wasn't following us.

Actually, the most memorable experience took place on the trip back north after Dad flushed, then opened our bathroom door. Remember the sewage treatment plant on Back River? Unfortunately, the attendant appeared at that moment to assemble our beds. We stepped into the aisle when she arrived and marveled at her speed.

"Geez," your father said. "She's like a commercial on fast forward." She was gone in no time. When she hurried past us in the aisle, we both looked down at our feet and mumbled, "Thank you."

"Oh, well," your father said, chuckling. "We'll never see her again."

As you know, Mike, we're patient people who enjoy reading and chatting, so waiting a total of ten hours while cars and passengers are loaded and off-loaded didn't bother us too much. I met a sweet lady who spent ten minutes bragging to me about her accomplished son, the dentist. But, really, how good could he be? The poor old dear seemed to be missing all of her teeth. And then there was eighty-year-old, recently divorced Larry, who is moving to Florida for the single women. "Oh, I'll be in great demand," he said, the morning sun reflecting off his head and his chest puffing out like he was Playboy of the month. We wished him well.

Anyway, Mike, we had a nice six weeks in Florida, but aren't sure if we'll be up for another Auto Train ride next year. So, we're considering spending next winter in San Francisco with you. We'll behave ourselves. Actually, we didn't break anything this year. Scott repaired the garage where your father backed into it last winter—just a small hole—and it turned out that the pile of melted plastic on the stove where I set the rubber pot was pretty easy to scrape off. The important thing is, we are all still on speaking terms. Think about it.

Love you,
Mom

P.S. I'm including my phone number in case you've misplaced it.

⇢ THE GOOD TIMES ⇠

*J*T'S SAD WHEN GROWN CHILDREN MOVE thousands of miles from home. Even when they assure you it's nothing personal, you have to wonder. Friends always try to make us feel better. "Well," they'll say, "at least you have interesting places to visit."

It's true that the kids do invite us. They even claim to enjoy our visits. But it's not the same as living around the corner from them.

We miss the children most of all on special occasions. Last Fourth of July, for instance, was filled with nostalgic reminiscing. Neighborhood celebrations were a big deal when the boys were young: swimming competitions at the YMCA Family Center, parades, games, and booming fireworks at Fullerton Field while the dogs cringed under our beds at home. And who could forget that homemade ice cream with fresh peaches or strawberries or pecans?

When John and I are feeling sentimental and missing our family, we take solace in the little things, like the treasured mementoes scattered about the house. They make the kids seem closer somehow and remind us of happy times. The tapestry pillow depicting a hunt scene on the sofa, for instance, and the white porcelain horse on the coffee table were gifts from Phil. Our youngest always did have a knack for choosing fun gifts. And when we need a laugh, we look at the painting of him in his cowardly lion costume.

There's a paperweight from a granddaughter's trip to Rome and a hand-decorated vase from another granddaughter—as well as a set of coasters from her wood etching days. We especially treasure the photographs on the walls, like the one of Scott's family taken aboard a cruise ship.

Son Mike's gifts have been a bit more exotic—kind of like his lifestyle. "What do you expect?" his father will say. "He's a kind-of *celebrity*—and you know how they are!" The chunk of petrified wood from Australia that's millions of years old, for example, and weighs more than the table it sits on. I considered it a labor of love that he lugged it thousands of miles in a suitcase. I don't let my husband pick it up. He has a hernia that groans when he lifts heavy objects.

The two sculptures in my writing room remind me of the international incident Mike caused when he was in Egypt. He was filming a show about tombs and mummies for the Discovery Channel when he awoke early one morning and went to his hotel window to investigate some noise. Seeing a bustling street market not far away, he quickly dressed and headed out in search of a souvenir or two.

In his haste, Mike forgot one incidental—his bodyguard—apparently a *big* deal in Cairo, especially for high-profile visitors. When security finally tracked him down and realized he hadn't been kidnapped, our son was carrying the two treasures which are now on my office desk. One is sand art—a lovely vase filled with colorful sand that spells out: *John loves Peg.*

The other is a sculpture. We don't know much about Egyptian art and culture and for a long time thought it was a bust of Queen Nefertiti. When John told Mike that the Egyptians have a strange idea of beauty, our son told us that it was King Tut. We appreciate it a lot more now. Anyway, it weighs five pounds and would make the perfect murder weapon in one of those PBS Agatha Christie mysteries.

Then there are the truly weird keepsakes—"conversation pieces"—Mike called them. We're the only ones in our friend group who have a biodegradable, eco-friendly cow pot—made of all natural cow manure—sitting on the dining room sideboard. I know, right? Some mothers get jewelry.

It came from a Connecticut dairy farm where Mike worked for one long day. He called us the morning it was to arrive in a UPS truck.

"It's a real work of art," he said, as though he was giving us a piece of fine crystal. "And it's *odorless*!"

Does my oldest son know me, or what? "Thanks, Mike," I said. "I've always been partial to the odorless knickknacks."

And then he said something you don't hear every day. "Inside the pot are some shiny, foil-wrapped treasures. *Do not let Dad eat them! They aren't chocolate covered cherries!* They're little balls of regurgitated body parts that owls cannot digest. You know—like bones, hair, and teeth. . . ."

We remember exactly when it arrived. As my husband likes to say, "It isn't every day UPS brings you a special delivery of owl vomit and cow shit." I saved Mike's card.

Mom and Dad,

Liven up your Fourth of July party with a game of "Name That Varmint." Have your friends reconstruct a rodent from the bones and teeth and hair inside the little owl pellets.

If this isn't to your liking, I have something special for my horse-loving mother—an attractive bottle of horse semen that would look great on the windowsill in the sunroom. It came from a famous quarter horse in Texas and could be a real conversation piece—especially in the morning sunlight where you can make out small clumps of dead sperm. Just let me know. I was saving

*that for Dad's next birthday. . . . Something to look forward
to, huh?*

Love, Mike

Thanks to his TV career, we're reminded of Mike often. The
night the sewage line broke in front of our condo, I thought of
him right away. When I stepped out of my car and saw trash in
the storm drain, there he was. One day I saw the word POOP
spray-painted on the highway overpass and remembered that our
oldest owed us a telephone call.

Like I said, it's sad when children move far away.

When my grandparents were elderly, they spent months at a
time visiting each of their children.

It's something to think about. . . .

I wouldn't want them to fight over us. . . .

⇢ FAMILY—A MIXED BLESSING ⇠

WE'VE ALL HEARD THOSE OLD PROVERBS: Children enrich our lives; Children are a comfort in our old age; Our children are a reflection of us.

My young husband and I were so gullible, we actually believed that propaganda. Who doesn't want some clone-like offspring? I had dreams of a big family and felt sorry for childless couples. What comfort and enrichment did they have to look forward to?

Three babies and five years later, my outlook was slightly more jaded. I came to the conclusion that twenty-seven months of pregnancy and nine months of morning sickness are quite enough of an investment in comfort and enrichment for our old age. What's more, the process known as *labor* is aptly named.

Fifty some years later, our sons have moved far, far away from their Baltimore home—and their parents. We hear from them once a week.

A recent Sunday was typical. Church, lunch at McDonalds with friends, then home to an Orioles game and our weekly phone calls from three middle-aged sons—children conceived in passion and devoted to enriching our lives.

The youngest, a free spirit who has always—as they say—marched to the beat of his own drummer, called during the third inning to inform us that he has decided to sell his few worldly possessions, put his three dogs in his van, and take to the road. He spoke these words to a father who worked the same job for thirty years, lived in the same house for forty years, has been married to the same woman for over fifty years, and has never done an impulsive thing in his life.

"It's about time I saw the world," he said. "I'll stop by in the fall, maybe for Thanksgiving." As he spoke, I was reminded of his words on a previous visit. John and I were engrossed in an eye-opening *Frontline* documentary on aging and senior care when he showed up at our door. He watched the last segment on nursing homes with us, then put his hand on my shoulder.

"Mom, you and Dad will never have to worry about being put in one of those places! You'll always have a home with me."

After my husband hung up on Sunday, he turned to me. "I'll flip you for the back seat."

Our oldest called during the seventh inning. Friends like to refer to him as the celebrity in the family, but the word *celebrity* has always had a glamorous connotation for me. Our son was on his way to Ft. Bragg, North Carolina, where he was scheduled to jump out of airplanes with the Army. Then he was going to participate in something called vertical dancing, which sounded kind of glamorous, until he explained that he would be dangling from the side of a tall building, suspended by a cable. The week before, he had called from a little town in Colorado called Craig, where he was castrating lambs the old-fashioned way—with his teeth.

I used to fantasize that he was calling to tell us he was getting married, but, of course, some things are way too scary.

Call me crazy, but I'm starting to think our kids don't have a handle on the whole "enriching our lives" concept.

Following another disappointing Orioles loss, our middle son called. John and I did most of the talking. Unlike my husband, engineers aren't famous for being chatty. But sometimes, if we ask just the right question, he'll tell us about his work—on the Miami tunnel project or the Lake Okeechobee Reservoir project. . . . Not that we understand a word of it, but it's fun to hear his enthusiasm.

"So, Scott, what did you do today?" his father will ask.

"I put the finishing touches on my new deck," he'll say.

"How's it look?"

"Marjie and the girls say they love it."

Or, "What do you and Marjie have planned for the weekend?" I'll ask.

"I have to go to Lowes for some parts."

"Oh yeah? So what project are you doing now?"

"I'm repairing the toilet," our son will say. Or, "I'm putting in a new sprinkler system." Or, "I'm replacing the kitchen faucets—or the ceiling fans." His father and I can only imagine. We hire professionals for repairs and projects.

On this particular Sunday, Scott had completely disassembled his John Deere tractor, replaced some parts, and reassembled it.

From time to time, my husband and I consider the possibility of having been given the wrong baby in the hospital—on three separate occasions.

Some days we're certain of it.

⇥ MY TRAVELING MAN ⇤

Dear Michael,

*D*ad enjoyed your Father's Day tribute on Facebook. The comments have been a welcome distraction from the stack of travel brochures beside his chair. I'm afraid your father's obsessed with taking another trip before he turns eighty-eight. I blame it on those nonstop river cruise commercials with the incredible scenery and inspirational music. He gets that dreamy look on his face every time he sees one, and I know exactly what's coming.

"Let's do this, Peg," he'll say. "Let's sail through the heart of historic cities and landscapes. Let's explore the world in comfort! Whaddaya say?"

Sometimes I just have to bring him back down to earth by reminding him that when it comes to traveling, we are jinxed! "John, have you forgotten our Mississippi River cruise?"

"That was years ago."

"Let me refresh your memory, hon," I say. "A plantation in Louisiana in July...105 degrees in the shade with 99 percent humidity and mosquitos the size of a Mississippi mud pie. Surely you remember the fried alligator nuggets and turtle soup that kept you in the bathroom all night."

I'm not sure exactly when it happened, Mike, but I've transformed from optimistic, adventurous explorer to reluctant traveler.

Whenever your father approaches me with a travel brochure, the theme music from Jaws plays in my head.

"We never go anywhere, Peg." I hear this ten times a day.

"John," I say, "look at the photographs on the wall. That's the Bridalveil Fall trail in Yosemite where I broke my foot running from a bear. I still have the X-rays and crutches and cast. And there's the lighthouse hostel in New York where we spent the night with four strange men and one bathroom because you said, "Oh hon, we've never stayed in a hostel before. Come on, it'll be fun!"

"Hey! It was romantic!" says your father. "The way the beacon flashed on and off . . . on and off . . . reflecting on the Saint Lawrence River."

He read that in a brochure! And I might add, Mike, that the beacon lit up the dormitory bedroom every ten seconds like an airport runway. Not that it mattered. It wasn't as though I intended to close my eyes.

"Well then, how about a cruise?" your father says. "Nothing bad ever happens on a cruise."

Instead of reminding him that hundreds of people have mysteriously disappeared from cruise ships over the years, I mentioned the thousands of travelers who recently retched for days, thanks to the Norwalk virus, and then there were the people who were stuck on some ship that ran aground. I might have also reminded him of our Alaskan cruise when it rained ten out of eleven days, and that New England and Canada cruise with seas so rough I felt like I had morning sickness all over again—for three days!

"It's not like you to be so negative, Peg. I know, how about a bus tour? They're easy and you see some terrific sites."

"You mean like our trip to Yellowstone? On the bus . . . off the bus . . . on the bus . . . off the bus, twenty times a day. Your back went out while we were watching Old Faithful the night before our raft trip down the Snake River. Surely you remember that!"

Fortunately, Mike, you can always count on a busload of seniors to be carrying enough drugs to stock a pharmacy. One woman even rubbed Dad's back with an Icy Hot substance and wrapped a bandage around his waist. I still remember that look of rapture! (On Dad's face, not the woman's.)

"By the time we reached the river, you were so jacked up on Vicodin and oxycodone, we had to tie you to the raft."

"We've been to Yellowstone...?"

Sorry if I sound heartless, Mike, but I'm still recovering from our trip home from Florida last Friday. The airport curse continues to hang over our heads like a storm cloud. When our 7:00 p.m. flight was cancelled, Dad insisted we sleep in the airport since the next flight was at 6:00 a.m. It made sense, sort of—although the Holiday Inn down the street was tempting.

"Are you sure it's safe?" I said. "It looks deserted, and I've heard stories about airports."

"Sure, it is. Come on hon, it'll be fun! Look, this couple's staying too."

The attractive younger couple were lugging two suitcases the size of Mini Coopers, plus two carry-ons and two shoulder totes.

"Geez," your father said to the man, clearly impressed. "You must have been on one of those around-the-world cruises, huh?"

The husband rolled his eyes. "A week at the beach." He pointed to a carry-on. "That one is mine."

"I have to be careful with luggage," Dad said, pointing to his abdomen. "Hernia."

Yes, Mike, your father is still hanging on to that hernia like it's a family heirloom. But that's another story.

Fifteen minutes later, we had staked out some cushioned chairs like a couple of homesteaders. Dad looked around and held out his arms like Ponce de León standing on the bow of a ship.

"Check this out, hon!" he said. "Palm trees, tropical plants, a trickling fountain, a charging station, and a bathroom just across the corridor. Who needs a Holiday Inn?"

While your father removed his shoes and hearing aids and settled down with a book, I took a walk to warm up and discovered that the tiny airport rolls up the runway at sunset. The corridor was like that scene from High Noon just before the duel. Not a soul in sight as far as the eye could see. Just empty chairs and closed restaurants and shops. Even the escalators had stopped running.

Back at the homestead, Dad was sprawled on a chair and covered with clothes from his suitcase as little puffs of steam came from his nostrils. He was snoring like a hibernating polar bear while arctic air poured down from the air conditioning vents in the ceiling. A baseball cap shielded his eyes from the bright overhead lights.

The younger couple, just twenty feet away, looked like an ad for a Sandals beach resort. Wrapped in thick, plush, colorful towels, she had pulled two chairs together and was sleeping peacefully. He was reading a book, sipping a drink, and using a jumbo suitcase as an end table.

I plopped in the chair across from Dad and pulled up my hood. Every fifteen minutes, announcements blared over the intercom.

"Welcome to Palm Beach International Airport. Beware of strangers who ask you to carry a package. Do not leave your bags unattended."

They were followed by a security guard on a Segway zipping along the corridor like a high-speed train, and loud chatter from the cleaning crew. Thanks to a nearby splashing fountain, I made frequent trips across the corridor to the ladies room. But that's okay. Sleep wasn't in my immediate future. I'm a person who requires a quiet, darkened room and a fluffy pillow.

Stay tuned, Mike. Our tour guide friend is planning a trip in the fall. Hopefully, it will be more successful than our river cruise which had to be cancelled due to—and get this—insufficient water in the

Danube River! Yep! A river without water. And your father refuses to admit that we are jinxed!

Now remember: our updated wills and advance directives are in the blue and white storage container on the closet shelf—just in case.

Love you,
Mom

P.S. I'm considering writing for a travel magazine, but your father thinks I need an attitude adjustment. What do you think?

MD
Mom

Hey Mike, planning trip to England! Watching PBS to learn language. Been trying to work "brilliant" into my conversation; the English love that one. I'd like to give "bugger" a try but need to do more research.

Expressions are tricky. If hotel clerk offers to come to my room in the morning to "knock me up," I won't be offended, and wild horses couldn't make me advise someone to "keep their pecker up," no matter how depressed they are.

Can't wait. Practicing my curtsey, just in case... Brilliant!

⇢ A PERFECT STORM ⇠

I WAS GETTING READY FOR CHURCH, PUTTING the finishing touches on my hair and face, when I noticed it. My jaw dropped, and I leaned toward the mirror for a closer look. After making a slight adjustment to my bra and the top of my robe, I hurried into the kitchen where my eighty-six-year-old husband was preparing our breakfast—yogurt, cereal, and fresh fruit.

"So, what do you think?" I asked, stepping in front of him, hands on my hips and shoulders back. He checked my hair and face, nodding in approval, then, as his head lowered, his eyes bugged out.

"Holy cow! Cleavage!" he said, locking me in an embrace and looking at the clock.

I've never been considered voluptuous—for a couple of reasons. And that was fine with me.

At school, I watched those well-endowed girls strutting through the hallways in their tight-fitting sweaters, flirting with boys. I had a theory about breast size and promiscuity, which explained my wholesome image.

Truth was, I was too obsessed with horses to be concerned about such things. In a time before sports bras, sitting the trot on a horse was more comfortable without five pounds of flesh flopping around like saddlebags and throwing me off-balance.

It was a different story after I discovered boys and dating. Suddenly I was envious of my buxom friends and fantasized about wearing those outstanding sweaters. In those days, brassieres were not softly rounded like those of today. Instead, they were cone-shaped—pointing ahead like some military weapon—and camouflaging one's natural contours.

My mother tried to be supportive, God love her. Her favorite "large-breasted" story was about her friend Kathy, who hadn't seen her stomach in twenty years and suffered from chronic upper back pain. I had seen for myself the indentations on Mom's shoulders from straps that had done double duty through the years.

Her stories of encouragement always ended the same. "You're better off on the small side, honey. When you get older, they just sag and get in the way. You take after your father's side of the family," she'd say, avoiding comparisons like grapefruit and lemons. And never once did she liken my chest to a midwestern prairie.

My husband has always been content with my God-given attributes— complimentary even. "They're just right," he'd say. "A nice handful." Is he the best, or what?

When I nursed our sons, I felt like Dolly Parton. I even wore the occasional sexy sweater, which, of course, was ruined with milk stains. After the babies were weaned, it was back to the slightly enhanced bra. Nothing extreme, mind you. Just enough to announce my presence.

At eighty-one, I'm with my husband—content with the way things are. From time to time I get lucky, and there's a "perfect storm" of underwear, outerwear, and flesh, that makes me feel like I'm in a Cialis ad. And who knows? I might get really lucky—and be late for church one Sunday.

→ THE FABRIC OF LIFE ←

OVER THE YEARS, MY HUSBAND HAS ACQUIRED a certain sartorial reputation. I wouldn't call him a clothes-horse exactly—or even a fashionista. But there's no denying he has style. If I had to give it a name, I'd go with Vintage Shabby.

John holds onto clothing like ordinary people hold onto family heirlooms. His closet is a museum of shirts and pants he brought to our marriage—like a dowry from over fifty years ago. They're safely hanging in our walk-in closet as if they're on the endangered species list.

My husband dressed appropriately for his teaching career, but when he retired, holey jeans and tattered shirts became the uniform of the day. Once, when he was in the middle of a messy home repair project, he announced that he needed something from Home Depot and picked up his car keys.

"What are you doing, John?" I said. "You can't go out in public like that!"

He looked down and brushed some dust from his shabby jeans. "Sure, I can. I'm dressing down—like kids do. Have you seen the stuff they wear?"

"You're dressing down?!" I asked him. "There's a hole in the seat of your pants the size of a sticky bun, John! I can see your white underwear! You get any more down, and you'll be arrested for indecent exposure."

"So? They're clean. You worry too much about what people think. I still remember that perfectly good pair of shoes you made me get rid of in London."

"Those 'perfectly good' shoes had soles that flapped like sheets on a clothesline in a windstorm. You left them on a hotel bed with a sign that said, 'Genuine leather. Enjoy!' "

"You'd like to dress me up like Rhett Butler, I guess." (We had just watched *Gone with the Wind* the night before.)

"Well, if people in the store offer you money, you'll see that I'm right!" I know a losing battle when I see one. Hanging on to the past is as much a part of John's psyche as his distrust of anything new—unless, of course, it comes from Goodwill.

I've seen the way our sons look at their father's outfits when they're home. Believe me, I've tried slipping a new garment among his "antiques" from time to time, only to see it shunned like a prostitute at a Sunday school picnic.

When we moved to a condominium in a slightly more upscale community, I made a point of discarding a few of my husband's more ragged garments. It wasn't easy, mind you. The two-step process began with hiding them for a month or so until they were forgotten. I was depending on the old adage "out of sight, out of mind." If their absence caused a spike in blood pressure, they would reappear magically at the bottom of a drawer. If not, they were placed in a garbage can and laid to rest.

Unfortunately, much of John's faded "dowry" sees the light of day far too often. Even birthday or Father's Day gifts from the children are regarded with disdain and viewed as excess.

"Oh, no!" he'll say, eyeing a delivery truck like it's a process server delivering a court summons. "This better *not* be something for me!"

On a recent morning, while John was working on our taxes, I gathered my coupons and headed to the mall for some end-of-season sales.

When I returned, John was at his office desk at the back of our bedroom. He stared at my shopping bag as though it might contain explosives—or worse still, something new and frivolous for him to wear.

"Look what I found," I said, taking a deep breath and reaching into the bag.

He backed off from the new shirt like it was fresh roadkill.

"I do not need another shirt! I have a closet full of shirts!"

"Which have been hanging there since shirts were invented." I stormed into the closet and returned with an armful of shirts, which I threw onto the bed.

"Just look at these frayed collars and sleeves, John! See these little fuzz balls? They're called pills, and they're holding your shirts together."

John hesitated, then said in a tone that could only be described as accusatory, "I guess you'd like to give them to Goodwill."

"Ha! That's a joke! Goodwill is not that desperate." And then I did quite possibly the gutsiest thing I've ever done in all our years of marriage. I opened my sewing basket, retrieved my sharpest pair of scissors, and cut off a collar, buttons, and sleeves.

John gasped, slapped his hand over his heart, and collapsed onto the bed.

"Oh, don't be so dramatic." I said. "It's not your sainted Aunt Louise; it's a faded shirt that's old enough for Social Security!"

He almost smiled, so with a stroke of genius, I added, "These are going to make the most awesome dust cloths ever. In fact," I said, putting my arm around his shoulder, "if you clear off your desk, I'll dust it with this very cloth right now. I know, we'll give some to the kids for Christmas. They'll think about you every cleaning day."

He gave me a peck on the cheek and headed back to his desk saying, "Don't overdo it, hon."

I have to say that convincing him was so easy, I almost regretted leaving the other bags in the car. Oh well, I could think about that tomorrow.

→ NOT OUR TURN ←

Hi Mike,

I'm still recuperating from the flu and in my downtime came across a lovely picture on the Internet of an elderly couple sitting on a green hillside looking into the sunset. It was an ad for a funeral home, and I said to myself, "Well, that could be Dad and me!"

Then I got to reminiscing over our exciting, albeit abbreviated, career in the world of television commercials. From Kimberly-Clark and Viva paper towels, to Lee jeans, to Discovery's Dirty Jobs and CNN's Somebody's Gotta Do It, we've had a ride for sure. Not to mention the recent Fel-Pro gaskets commercial and appearances on Returning the Favor. What fun we've had working with our kid. Even when we got paid only in steamed crabs.

So I'm thinking maybe you could use your considerable "pull" to get us another commercial—for a funeral home, perhaps. It's a subject on which your father and I have a great deal of expertise. We've spent more time in funeral homes than in doctors' offices—and that's saying something. As a matter of fact, we know all the staff at the local establishments, and they know us—kind of how the people on Cheers knew Norm and Cliff.

I recently had an interesting encounter with the owner of a funeral home we were visiting for the first time. While your father was busy reminiscing with some old teacher friends, I wandered back to the office and peeked through the door. I love engaging people in conversation—especially those with interesting jobs. It must have been a slow night, because the woman smiled and waved me in. You don't ordinarily expect funeral directors to look happy, probably out of respect for the grieving.

We chatted for a minute, and when I learned that she was the owner of the establishment, I said, "I imagine you've had some interesting experiences through the years." She got up and closed the office door as though she was about to divulge some dirt on a corrupt local official, or maybe describe some new embalming procedure. But it was even better. Boy, did I get an earful. I heard about a feuding family that came to blows right there at the foot of the casket holding the deceased. "They practically knocked it over," she said. "One of the guys ran outside, and I was afraid he was going for a weapon, so I called the police; the station is right across the street. They showed up in riot gear—with tear gas!"

We had a good laugh and when we finished, she launched into a story about a deceased woman who hated her two greedy daughters-in-law.

"She left directions in her will to be buried in her full-length sable coat so they wouldn't get it. It was worth a fortune! We had to hire a security guard for two days!" We laughed again, and I knew I would be making notes on the way home so as not to forget the stories.

Like your father says, "Another week, another funeral." They're always sad, of course. But at our age, they're often a celebration of life. Twice we had two funerals in the same week. As we were leaving the viewing, your father shook his head and sighed.

"Sometimes I feel like we're in one of those documentaries Mike narrates for the National Geographic channel. We're in a herd of migrating wildebeests crossing a Serengeti river. And the crocodiles are ravenous." Then he turned to me and said, "Guess it wasn't our turn today. How about a crab cake?" Your father is a philosophical kind of guy.

Our church offers a funeral luncheon for members. It's a wonderful event that is so much warmer and more personal than in a restaurant where everybody stays seated, and you feel rushed. I usually take my baked bean casserole; in fact, some people call me the Bean Lady. The dish is probably better suited to outside picnics, though, where there's a little breeze. But if the weather's nice enough to open the windows, they're fine for indoor funeral luncheons.

Naturally, Dad and I have become accustomed to funeral home protocol over the years—the sign-in sheet and memorial cards, the casket, flowers, family, friends, pictures, and digital slideshows. A section of our closet is designated exclusively for funeral clothes. I wear a pair of dark slacks and shoes, with a jacket that has a little color in it. No shocking-pink or fire-engine red, of course! It is, after all, a somber atmosphere.

Not that your father strictly observes subtle colors. He's more a "come as you are" kind of person. The day he removed his coat and revealed a Porky Pig necktie, I felt lightheaded. But Dad shrugged and said, "Hey, it's a celebration of life. Nothing says celebrate like a dancing pig, right?" I have to pick my battles with your father.

I'm always careful to turn off my phone before I enter the funeral home, especially if there's a service in progress. I learned that lesson from my cousin Nancy. At my father's funeral, she thought her phone was turned off when she put her purse on the floor beneath the pew. But during the solemn eulogy, it rang. She picked it up, dropped it, and the darn thing vibrated out of reach. It traveled all the way up to the next pew while playing two verses of "Yankee Doodle."

Nancy could barely hold up her head at the luncheon afterward, but relatives tried to make her feel better. Cousin Straughan said, "Nancy, that was a perfect selection. After all, Uncle Carl was a Yankee who came to Virginia to ask for Aunt Thelma's hand." Even my mother tried to comfort my cousin. "Well, Nancy, your Uncle Carl had a sense of humor. He would have laughed." Even so, I never want to be in that position.

I usually sign the guest book as soon as we arrive, then we make our way to the casket. One always speaks softly, as a sign of respect. I always try to be positive in my comments, "Oh, doesn't she look nice?" I'll say. Or, "She looks so natural, as though she's just napping." Your father thinks I overdo it.

"Geez, Peg," he says, "by the time you leave, the family expects her to sit up and sing a chorus of 'Everything's Coming Up Roses.' " Dad can be sarcastic. So I reminded him of the time he tried to find something nice to say about old Tom when he passed. To his credit, he didn't mention that Tom had died in the arms of another man's wife. Instead, Dad looked at the family and with a straight face, said, "Boy, that Tom always had a lot of energy, didn't he?" When he added, "Yes sir, he lived life to the fullest, right up to the climax," I had to cover my face with my handkerchief.

Anyway, Mike, that's how it used to be at funeral homes—somber and respectful—except for the occasional dancing pig. But now, visiting a funeral home, in the words of your father, is an absolute crapshoot. Thanks to you and your career, we never know what to expect!" The first time we experienced the Mike Rowe effect was at Peaceful Destinations after an old childhood friend had passed. I hadn't seen the family in years. Dad agreed to accompany me and was signing the guest book when we heard the scream. Things were subdued when we entered, so I assumed the scream was someone's extreme expression of grief and angst.

"Look! It's Miss Peggy!" a woman yelled, rushing toward me with open arms. It was my old friend's daughter. "We just love, love your son!" She was followed by a brother and then the widow. People stopped their conversations and watched as for the next half hour, the family relived their favorite episodes of Dirty Jobs, recounting them to us as though we had never seen the show. Not that it isn't fun to hear people proclaiming the genius of our eldest. But really? In a funeral home? When a grandson said, "Did you see the one where Mike was crawling through the sewers and a roach ran down his pants?" an elderly aunt laughed so hard she spit her dentures out, had an asthma attack, and had to be carried to a chair and given her inhaler.

When Dad and I left, without even making it to the casket, we were followed to the door by family and friends, still laughing and talking about our clever son.

"Well, that was weird," I said.

"Yeah, but at least we left them in good spirits. How about a crab cake?" Leave it to your father to put a good spin on it.

That was nothing compared to our experience at the Tranquil Alternatives funeral home. Ordinarily we go to the 3:00 to 5:00 p.m. visitation but had decided on the 7:00 to 9:00 p.m. this time in hopes of seeing some old college friends. We hadn't seen the deceased since school days. He had been a pompous kind of guy—always had to be the center of attention and, from what we'd heard, hadn't changed through the years. Even now, his golden urn stood on an altar with a spotlight on it, surrounded by what looked like a victory garland wreath. Things were tranquil with soft music in the background. We spoke to the family and reconnected with old friends. But, thanks to a Dirty Jobs marathon that day, Tranquil Alternatives was about to become a little less tranquil.

From the corner of my eye, I saw the wheelchair moving in our direction. "Hey, I know you! You're Mike Rowe's parents, aren't you?"

"Guilty," your father said, as he usually does in that situation. The elderly gentleman applied his brake and lurched to his feet saying in a gruff, booming voice, "Well, I just saw your son on television. He was standing in shit up to here." He drew an imaginary line across his chest, then broke out in hysterical laughter. He was joined by others and, just like that, the seal was broken with everyone discussing the details of your most disgusting jobs.

The golden urn—no longer the center of attention—had become an insignificant prop in the laughter-filled room, as I imagined a swirling dust storm of ashes within. When we left, your father observed, "Oh, well, I guess it wasn't our turn today, hon. You fancy a crab cake?"

Anyway, no pressure, Mike, but if you ever get an actual agent, we're still available to do a commercial and willing to work for food.

Love you,
Mom

→ THE WANDERING RECLUSE ←

Dear Mike,

*P*lease don't sit around feeling guilty about not making it home for your father's birthday. He understands your busy schedule, and I assure you he's quite content. He's an eighty-five-year-old man who thinks he's Peter Pan.

I try to keep my sense of humor. The other morning when I turned on the bathroom light and exclaimed, "I hate mirrors!" your father said, "What do you expect? You're eighty years old. Flowers fade…grass withers…leaves turn brown and crinkle…riverbeds dry up…"

"All right!" I said, throwing my tube of age-defying moisturizer at him. "I get the point!" Don't worry; I threw it way over his head. You can't take chances with somebody on a blood thinner.

Just as I slammed the door behind me, the phone rang, and Dad answered it on speaker, since he didn't have his "ears" in yet.

It was the office of his long-time cardiologist. You know, the one with the shapely receptionist famous for short skirts and plunging necklines. I remember the first time I saw her. Everybody does. When I questioned the wisdom of such a wardrobe in a practice that treats men with weak hearts, your father said, "Are you kidding? She's a pacemaker on heels. No man's heart is going to stop with her in the room." As an afterthought, he added, "Besides, she's darned efficient."

Naturally, I couldn't help overhearing Dad's phone conversation through the widening crack in the door.

"All right, sweetie, it's a date," said the darned-efficient pacemaker on heels. "I'll see you next Tuesday at 1:30."

"Thanks, hon," said your father. "You're on my calendar." I couldn't see his face, but I could hear the smile in his voice. What is it about old men? People can't do enough for them.

It's the same thing when he volunteers at the hospital. At dinner I have to listen to him rave over a soothing neck massage or invigorating quickie backrub from nurse Edna, or Joyce, or Sandra. I don't really mind; it's kind of nice to see that dreamy look again. As you know, Mike, I've never been the jealous type. Though I admit to being shocked when I stopped at the theater dressing room the other evening to give your father his glasses. He was pulling on a pair of trousers while actresses ran around in their underwear—just slips, panties, and bras. Really!

"Men and women use the same dressing room?" I asked. He merely grinned and shrugged. "What can I say? It's the arts."

The show was Social Security, and Dad played a ninety-eight-year-old artist who was having an affair with an eighty-year-old widow. His favorite line was, "For a hundred-year-old Jew, I look terrific!" I had to remind him that it's because he's really only eighty-four.

On another note, I came across an article online the other day you might find interesting. Perhaps you've already heard this, but according to Hindu doctrine, there are four stages of life. Given his age, your father should be entering stage three: Vanaprastha, or the Hermit in Retreat stage. His children and grandchildren have established lives of their own. The time has come to renounce physical and material pleasures, retire from social and professional life, leave his home, and go to live in a forest hut. He is, though, allowed to take his wife along.

Fortunately, we're Presbyterian, where stage three is less clearly defined. It's the one where wives are obsessed with the deterioration of their bodies, while their husbands are busy being adorable to the opposite sex.

Anyway, Mike, it's fortunate that we do not belong to the Hindu faith. Your father would be bored to tears in a forest hut. Take the other day, for instance. We were enjoying the forbidden fruit at Five Guys when a woman walked in. There was a jewel in her navel the size of the Hope Diamond and a ring through her nostrils that could have come from my shower rod. The red streak in her hair matched a tattoo on her neck. Oh! And she had a serious limp. And still, your father couldn't take his eyes off her.

One thing for sure: whether you're a Hindu or a Presbyterian, stage three is not for sissies! I'm just saying...

So don't waste your time feeling guilty about Dad's birthday, Mike. Besides, we have plans. I hope this won't be TMI, but your father has threatened to treat me to some heavy breathing for the occasion. That is if we're up for it! I can't remember the last time we took a power walk around the park together.

Just so you know, I read somewhere that stage four in the Hindu faith is known as Sannyasa. Apparently, some people refer to it as the Wandering Recluse stage.

Stay tuned!

Love,
Mom

✦ MATERIAL MAN ✦

*T*ODAY BEGAN LIKE MOST DAYS—WITH JOHN fixing himself a bowl of cereal, or rather, *cereals*.

I thought back to the last time one of our sons was in town. He had chuckled as his father poured cereal from four different boxes into a bowl.

"So, what do you call that concoction?"

John shrugged. "Uh, Cheerie-Capt'n-Total-Os? It's good; have some." Our son declined.

One morning recently, as John was diving into his cereals, I answered the phone to learn that a salesman from a large investment company had a deal for me.

"Hold on a minute, I have just the person for you," I told him.

My husband loves salesmen. Nothing puts us on a Do-Not-Call list faster than a few minutes with *Mr. Perry Mason* himself. I handed over the phone while covering the mouthpiece.

"Here you go, hon—a little red meat with your cereal." John put the phone on speaker, and I listened, smiling.

"So where are you calling from, son?" he asked, crunching his concoction. "Yeah? What's the weather like in Philadelphia? Uh-huh. You a baseball fan? The Orioles are having another good year. So, what do you think of that mayor of yours?"

Later, as John was preparing to leave for his Wednesday senior group, he said, "My, that was a nice young man. His last name was Harrison, but his mother was a Klausmeyer. He might be related to the Klausmeyers down the street. Small world!"

At the front door, I conducted my exit interview, brown bag lunch in tow.

"Cell phone?"

"Check," John said, tapping his jacket pocket.

"Hearing aids?"

"Huh?"

"Very funny!" I said.

"Tooth?"

He smiled, revealing his upper plate with one tooth. "Check."

"Foot brace?"

He lifted his pant leg. "Check."

"Wallet?" He patted his back pocket.

"Glasses?"

"On my nose."

We laughed. As I handed him his lunch, he gave me a peck on the cheek.

"And what are you going to do today?" John asked, adjusting his Orioles cap.

"Oh, I have to write a blog."

My husband shook his head. "It's amazing how you're always able to come up with material. I don't know how you do it."

A minute later as I sat at my computer, the phone rang, and it was *guess who*. I retrieved his car keys from the table by the door. (I must be slipping.)

"Have a good day," I said, dropping them over the balcony railing and into John's waiting hands. "Love you!"

"Me too."

Material indeed!

→ AFTERWORD ←

by John Rowe

I'VE LEARNED A LOT ABOUT MARRIAGE OVER the past sixty years. Mainly, that it's all about change.

In 1960, the only entrées my wife could cook were hot dogs and grilled cheese sandwiches—which were occasionally burned. And the only things she ironed were the fronts and collars of my shirts—which were also occasionally burned.

When we started a family, I was the breadwinner while Peg stayed at home with the kids. Those were the good old days.

Eventually, my wife was like Martha Stewart, cooking three course breakfasts and ironing entire shirts so that I could remove my jacket at work. She even made time to help me learn lines and attend all my plays in local theatrical productions.

And then at the age of eighty, Peg decided to write a book. I could say, "And that's all she wrote," but it would be a lie. Because now she has written a second book and tells me she's working on her third.

But that's okay because, as I say, marriage is about change. I've learned to cook breakfast and the cleaners across the street does a decent job on dress shirts—fronts and backs. Peg doesn't have a lot of time for helping me with lines or attending plays these days. But that's no longer an issue, since finding roles for an eighty-seven-year-old man is nearly impossible.

So now I get to follow my wife around to book events. It's kind of fun since I'm a star on social media myself. And I've been led to believe that this book is going to make me even more famous. The question is: Will I be able to show my face in public?

Like I say, marriage is all about change.

→ IMPORTANT PEOPLE: MY LFBF ←

*S*EVERAL YEARS AGO, MIKE ENCOURAGED ME to write a book—so I did. Then he encouraged me to join Facebook. So I did. Did I like it? No! Quite the opposite, in fact. It was work!

Then a funny thing happened. People began reading my meanderings on my @TheRealPeggyRowe Facebook page and sharing with friends. They responded to my blogs and made interesting, often humorous, comments. I know this because I actually read and respond to many of them. It's no longer work, but a place to meet friends over some happy, humorous, and poignant stories.

Now I've written a second book, and my publisher has made a request: "For the back cover, we should have some reviews or recommendations. Who are some public figures or important people that you especially admire, Peggy? I'll contact them."

My response: "Well, when it comes to people I respect, my Little Facebook Friends (LFBF) come to mind. Perhaps they'd be willing to give a testimonial about my writing; that would encourage others to pick up my new book."

And that's just what they did! There were so many, in fact, that we ran out of space long before we ran out of comments. Perhaps we could use them for my next book…

Thanks to all the "important people" in my life. You really are the best!

Lizmari Brignoni Airdo Mrs. Rowe is a skillful storyteller who brings you along in her journey. You will relate to her stories or might even feel that you're part of them!

Barbara Coty Anthenat Peggy's storytelling makes the mundane seem special. She handles difficult parts of life as opportunities. Being a part of her life through her writings is a unique adventure.

Janet DeJesus Jose Arambulo The moment you were introduced to "Old Blue," you wanted to learn more about Mike's mom, Peggy! Peggy has a unique gift of "painting a life experience." Peggy takes you with her to revisit her world, sharing normal life experiences, giving you an up-close and personal account with infinite details. Peggy takes in every moment with poise and lots of laughter. Her candid writing, humor, and wit allow the reader to have a birds-eye view of an event, using words to paint a picture of a life well lived.

Carol Wesolowski Black Peggy's stories remind us of how good people live good lives. Common sense, generosity, a simple enjoyment of family, friends, and community told in very captivating way. Not since Erma Bombeck has there been such a witty author who puts a smile on my face and a warmth in my heart.

Sean Hays Arter I've loved Peggy Rowe's writing since I listened to her son read her emails in his podcasts. She has the gift of finding humor in the mundane and of slipping some inspiration in with it. I can honestly say I have loved everything I've read (or heard) that she has written.

Thelma Ebert Beamon Now we know where TV's Mike Rowe gets his unique sense of humor—from his mom, Peggy Rowe! Her take on life is hysterical and a great way to look at everyday issues with a sense of humor. Peg, hope your second book is as successful as your first. Of this I have no doubt... 🖤

Jan Belote Peggy Rowe's writing skill envelops the reader with sense of time and place, gently amusing without making fun of her subjects. She finds the best in everyone who crosses her path and draws you into her world, leaving you with warmth and peace.

Shari Boyd There is no one better to share a cup of tea with than Peggy Rowe. Her stories, her humor...everything just keeps you engaged and turning the page...like the days of Ann Landers, Dear Abby, and Erma Bombeck, we now have the incredible Miss Peggy to add to the list.

Sonja Bethy Ario Funny, slightly naughty, uplifting, and warm-hearted. Everything we need in this day and age! Keep writing and teasing your kids and husband and sharing it with us. We love it! 😍

Bonnie Ohlert Bowman She is your mom, your favorite aunt, that schoolteacher you loved to listen to, your sister, and your best friend all rolled into one, just having tea and telling stories.

Diane Brazier Peggy Rowe is everyone's mom, grandma, sister, aunt. At least she is for me. When I read her books, I hear my mother's voice. The laughter and smiles those memories bring are priceless—and so is Peggy. The writing gene is strong in this family, and I predict that in the very near future people will be saying, "Mike Rowe? Isn't he Peggy Rowe's son?"

Marilynn Breiner *About My Mother* has given me smiles and some tears as it brings back beautiful memories that I shared with my momma who passed away 10 years ago of Alzheimers.

Judi Brooks Your book made me smile 😊 when life was difficult. You truly have a gift to tap into bringing humor and light to life.

Karen Swetonic Brooks Peggy Rowe's sharp but gentle humor and quirky insights on living your best life have inspired a host of followers to take a fresh look at life with a dash of humor. Well done, Miss Peggy!

Mary Boudman Peggy lives life as we all do—one common event after another. Only she tells it with the best words...words that make us realize how great each and every day can be.

Ellen Bunnell When I pick up a new book, I expect to be entertained. I rarely expect to be taken back to my childhood where I laugh, cry, remember people I love, and appreciate the simple life. Peggy Rowe does all this using a delightful writer's method: simple storytelling.

Cathy Burk Peggy Rowe's stories feel like a warm, nostalgic hug. She had us hooked from the time Mike read us the saga about her Big Blue Purse getting lost at Walmart! Her first book was a joy to read for anyone who ever had a mother! Thank you, Peggy, for giving us more delightful stories to look forward to.

Davena Burns-Peters Reading Peggy's daily writings bring a smile to my face and uplifts my heart. I look forward to the brief time to laugh, reflect, and be in awe about life with her. Peggy's writing is a bright spot and makes the world just a little bit brighter.

Sarah James Carlson Peggy's writing warms your heart, brings joy and laughter, and reminds us of the beauty of life that can be found in our everyday circumstances. She shows us all that the gift of a life lived well is worth sharing.

Veronica Cavallero Happy, uplifting, insightful...all describe the writings of Mrs. Rowe. She's a shiny gem in this sometimes dull and dreary world we live in. Grab a coffee or tea and sit a bit... you'll be glad you did!

Barb Daley Cheek Genuine, hilarious, and heartwarming... Peggy Rowe knows how to tell a story and make you feel as if you aren't reading it but are listening to her tell you over a cup of tea. Simply joyful!

Valerie Hurley Conger Peggy Rowe's writings make me smile. Whether it's her book *About My Mother* or her Facebook posts, she brings an honesty and caring to her writings that warms your heart. She is truly an inspiration.

Grace Marie Conley Life with Peggy and John brightens up an otherwise dim newsfeed. She has a unique perspective of life and all of its gritty, funny, and poignant details.

Jeannie Crawford Down to earth, funny, touching, a story written in a way that the reader feels compelled to finish all at once and go back to read again and again. I'm looking forward to her next book and the many ones after that.

Andrea Cyr Your writing makes me feel as if I am there. You clearly articulate the trials and tribulations of the parent/child relationship with humor and candor. It was a pleasure to read your book, and I look forward to the next one.

Julie Annedora Daniels Mom's got a lighthearted look at life with a serious sense of humor. She makes me smile inside and out.

Terri Faulkner DeMasellis Refreshingly honest, heartfelt, and whimsical, Peggy Rowe waxing nostalgic is a feel-good read! You will be entertained by the way she spins an ordinary day into a wonderful piece of art! She engages the reader to see with clarity, and inviting you to use all of the senses. Gloriously beautiful. ~Blessings~

Penny Donnell As soon as you start reading you feel like one of the family...so honest, so heartwarming! An overwhelming testament that life is not necessarily over at 80, just a new beginning... so encouraging!

Kelly Eddy I could not wait to get my hands on Peggy's book. When her son would read letters she had written I would cry from laughing. Her book—fun, funny, loving—does not disappoint. Way to go, Peggy!

Angela Edens Peggy Rowe's writing is honest, humorous, and relatable. She touches your heart with her experiences, memories, and thoughts on life. She reminds you to see the positive and enjoy the ride! Thanks for sharing so openly with your LFBF. 😊

Michelle Pisapia Egan Peggy is anything but boring!! She has an ability to write a story that brings a smile to your face, warmth in your heart, and sometimes a tear to your eyes. Anyone who can tell a story like that is worth reading.

Joy Colter Fitzpatrick She's the Erma Bombeck of this era. She's funny and honest and so entertaining and witty. I just love her!

Trish Cash Flynn Peggy Rowe is such a great storyteller that you can't help but be swept into her stories. The way she writes, you feel all the emotions along with her. She is such a blessing!

Diane Phillips Foster Wonderful book, filled with charming memories, humor, grit, and love. It will touch your heart, and make you wish you'd grown up with Peggy.

Chaye Goodrich I read your book while my husband was healing from a knee replacement & I laughed out loud in the waiting room of the physical therapy office quite often. I gave it to my uncle for a laugh while he goes for cancer treatments. I can't wait for your next book. ☮💜📚

Joanne Griffin If it were a season, Peg's writing is Summer. The pace is unhurried, like a cool brook through the overgrowth of overheated vacation reads. It is all of one long Summer with a few passing clouds. Pure delight!

Natalie Guthrie Reading Peggy's stories is like having coffee with a dear friend. You laugh a lot while simultaneously feeling part of her family. You come away smiling and feeling refreshed.

Becky Harris Mrs. Rowe has written a funny, fast-moving book that inspired me to look at my life with my mom through the lens of humor. What a gift.

Rosemarie Till Hawthorne Reading Mrs. Rowe's book is like sitting down for a cup of tea with your most interesting friend; her stories just come pouring out! Can't wait for your next book!

Melissa Herron Peggy's stories remind us that we are all human and should find the joy and humor in everyday life. Move over, Mike, there is another Rowe who is shining bright!

Cindy Jetton Peggy Rowe is one of the rare, talented authors who has you hooked from the first page and sad whenever it is the last page. She is a MUST-read author.

Karen Huizing Inman Reading Peggy's stories is like sitting down for coffee with your favorite relative. It is taking ordinary moments and turning them into ones you cherish and hold close to your heart.

Kathy Schulz Kiran Peggy's books are what you read (repeatedly) when you want to be inspired by someone who has mastered the art of finding the silver lining in every situation.

Mary Kistler Having met the Rowes in person, and having read the first edition of Peggy's book, all I can say is, I can't wait to read this next entry into the literary world. May she write enough to fill a library!

Maggie Kriz Move over Mike Rowe. Thanks to your encouragement, you & your brothers now get to share your mom with her legion of Little Facebook Friends. Peggy Rowe brightens our lives by sharing her wit, wisdom, and gratitude with us. We are a lucky bunch, indeed!

Jeanny Laurie I hung on to every single word and was delighted by every single page of the book. Peggy took me back in time and let me peek into her family history. I did not want the book to end...and cannot wait to read the second book!!!!

Melodee Mefford Peg's humor and writing are really a testament to a life lived well, with grace and no small measure of life's craziness. Highly recommend this book!

Helen Jones Leonard I am not much of a writer, but I just love what you write about and how you write...perfect words. Thank you for sharing your gift! Inspiring, uplifting, hilarious.

Paula Martino McCutcheon Peggy takes the mundane, normal, everyday thing and makes me laugh! If you loved Erma Bombeck, you will love Peggy Rowe! She makes you feel good through and through!

Colleen Ahearn Mckerley Peggy Rowe is a writer everyone can relate to and brings a lighthearted joy to reading about her adventures even if it is only to Walmart with her husband, Prince Charming. You will laugh, cry, and remember a day when we all said "Hello" to our neighbor.

Gail Bryan Mitchell Thanks to Mike Rowe for sharing his mom with the rest of the world. Peggy provides laughter and love in all of her stories and makes you feel like part of her family. Her writing, like her memories, is impeccable, and I look forward to all of her books and posts!

Carol Krieger-Lowe Morganroth Peg's hilarious anecdotes about ordinary life are all you need to find your smile each day. She's a gem!

Lisa Payne Morley Thank you for reminding us that love is both enduring and fun! Your amazing wit and awesome sense of humor are exactly what this world needs more of! Looking forward to reading this book as much as I did the first one! Sincerely, ALFBF

Leslie Orthober This amazing woman inspires young and old alike with everything she writes. I know this anxiously awaited book will be awesome just like Peggy is.

Medeann Parton *About My Mother* is a beautiful, well written look into the life of a strong, funny, and talented lady. I still find myself thinking of bits and pieces from it when I'm at a ball game, caring for a friend's horse, or just spending time with my own mother.

Lorrie Patton Peggy Rowe, your book is an awesome read. You and your "sidekick" keep me entertained and laughing, and even a few tears. Oh, to have your spunk and spirit when I reach your age; oh wait, I'm there!!?

Kristy Ruppert Pelletier Today the world seems to be all about electronics, so *About My Mother* is a breath of fresh air. This delightful gem takes us back to a simpler time where relationships mattered, and family comes first. Written by Peggy Rowe, America's mom or grandma, you'll feel like you are sitting at the kitchen table just reminiscing.

Janice Peterson Peggy is a blessing to all of us. She makes you stop and appreciate the little mundane things of life with renewed hope, wonder, and appreciation. You will never regret reading her work.

Cindy Leath Peggy's stories are funny, witty, honest, and she is completely relatable to any age group. She touches on subjects that we have experienced or probably will some day. I've been brought to snorts of laughter and to quiet tears reading Peggy's words.

Christi Smith Reistad Reading Peggy's words of wisdom about life's ups and downs always brings a smile to my face. Reading is a way to understand life and doing it with Peggy is a joy.

Christina Rhymer Peggy Rowe's light and lively wit takes the ordinary and makes it extraordinary—extraordinarily funny, that is!

Tammy Richardson No one can tell a story like Peggy Rowe! Her books appeal to all ages. She always brings a smile and a lot of LOLs to my day!

Roberta McMills Rohwer I doubt when she began that Peggy Rowe intended to give Erma Bombeck a run for her money! But that's what she did, and then some! I, and millions of others, felt like we're once again home...in a cozy kitchen, listening to our mothers and grandmothers tell stories! It was wonderful! We cried..we laughed...we remembered, and that made us capture the good...even if just for a little while!

Laura Schofield I always take a pause to read what Peggy Rowe has written, no matter how busy my schedule. It is always thoughtful, often funny, and full of the wisdom that this girl stationed far away from family misses hearing from her own grandmothers, aunts, and mother.

Barbara Schwab Delightful and insightful, Peggy Rowe can make even the most mundane humorous. She is delightfully honest and hilarious. She makes you feel like you are her friend.

Joann Siccardi In today's crazy world, Peggy Rowe's words are a sound reminder to approach everything with a touch of grace and a lot of humor. Bringing inspiration to many that it's never too late to try something new. You never know where you might end up, even on the NYT bestseller list!! Thank you for all the smiles!!!!

Leslie Skibitsky Peggy Rowe is Everywoman—at least the way Everywoman would like to be. Everywoman's life isn't perfect, but she does her best to find humor, meaning, and love in life every day.

Kathy Smith Peg Rowe brings such truth, humor, and smiles to the realities of life. There is not a moment that she shares that doesn't resonate with those of us walking through this experience called Life!

Lisa St.Romain Reading Peggy Rowe's book has reminded me that it's the little things in life that matter most and the wonderful memories that you make along the way! It also reminded me that when it comes to family, patience is truly a virtue! Her style of writing is laugh-out-loud funny and heartwarming; you won't be disappointed!

Lori Strouse I am even more confident in reaching my golden years because *About My Mother* has shown me the way with her grace, poise, and wisdom during her tribulations and celebrations in life, family, and community.

Jamie Hill Sweadner Peggy writes in such a way that makes me want to sit down and have coffee and pie with her. I feel like I know her as I know other dear friends. Her love of life, friends, and family is heartwarming, and her telling of stories brings both tears and laughter. I'm forever grateful to her son, Mike, for encouraging Peggy to share her world with us.

Ruth Szpunar Peggy Rowe is one of the funniest writers I've ever read. She can make you howl with laughter at the ordinary stories of life. But she's also poignant and real—you know that she's a real person, with real struggles, just like the rest of us. As a librarian, this is one author who always gets a 5-star review and recommendation from me!

Juli Hansen Tesmer Thank you for reminding us that humanity is real, living, and thriving at any age. That simplicity of life is the largest gift we can bring to others.

Pam Vloedman Verhagen I've never met Peg, but I know her so well. She is all of us rolled in to one sweet package with unbelievable wit and charm. I smile at every word she writes.

Christine Veirs Peggy Rowe writes from the heart with joy, laughter, and a bit of wisdom. She's Young in Heart, and we love her and her writing!!

Michele Wallace It's a smile around every corner when you're walking alongside Peggy. Sage musings and indispensable wit for a brighter world. LFBF from DE

Melinda White Honest, relatable, hilarious—Peggy Rowe knows exactly how to tell a story in a way that leaves a reader wanting to be her best friend! Her stories about her family make me remember my moments of craziness with my own family and remind me to always cherish those precious memories.

Michele Bunds Williams Peggy Rowe's love for her family is palpable in all her writings. Her stories resonate with that love, spiced with humor. She allows the reader to see their own family in a new light and to love and appreciate them anew.

Brittany Woods This was my favorite book I've read in a long time. Such heartwarming, funny stories! I was often in tears...the sad ones and the happy ones! Peggy Rowe knows how to tell a story so that you feel like you're right there with her. I've recommended this book to everyone I know!

Teresa Wyckoff Peggy Rowe's writing style is laugh out loud on public transportation awesome!

Two different worlds.
John and Peggy—1960

He's in the Army now!
19-year-old Private Rowe—1952

She didn't know the gun was loaded.
Celebrity Thelma Knobel—1953

I'm still pinching myself.
John and Mike—1962

Two and counting.
Mike, John, and Scott—1966

The Rowe boys.
Scott, Mike, Phil, and John—1976

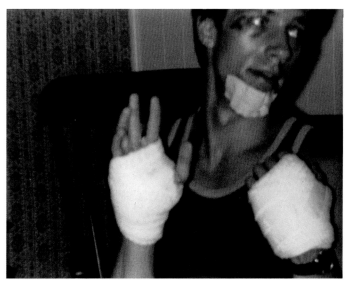

A bad day on the garbage truck.
Mike—1980

One down, two to go!
John, Mike, Phil, and Scott Rowe and Carl (Pop) Knobel—1980

So pretty! "Semi-Fourmals" Barbershop Quartet.
Mike Rowe, Bob Coffman, Chuck Klausmeyer, and Mike Price—1980

There's a new sheriff in town.
John in *The Rainmaker*—1988

A roaring celebrity.
Phil Rowe as the Cowardly Lion in *The Wizard of Oz*—1983

And that makes three!
Phil and John Rowe—1985

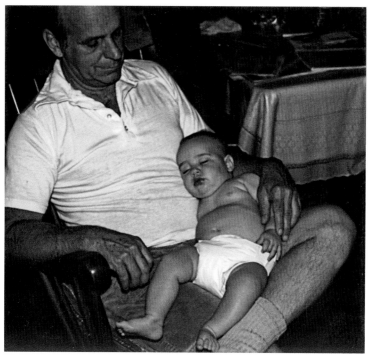

Babysitting's a piece of cake.
John and Katie—1987

A princess.
Scott, Katie, and John—1987

Happy Birthday, firstborn.
Best man Mike, Marjie, and Scott Rowe—1988

Ready for his celebrity headshot.
Mike—1989

Dressing room Romeo.
John—1992

Scott and his girls.
Scott, Marjie, Katie, and Jessie Rowe—1995

John and Peggy along the way—1993

Christmas socks.
Jessie, Katie, and Grandad—2006

A curtain call.
John and cast—circa 2000

All in a day's work.
Retiree John—1995

From country to condo.
The Rowe Family—2001

The Lighthouse *"hostile."*
John and Peggy—2007

In the company of heroes.
Peggy and John—2008

Canada by train.
Peggy and John—2011

Feeling no pain.
John on a Snake River raft—2009

Ready for our close-up.
The Rowe Family—2010

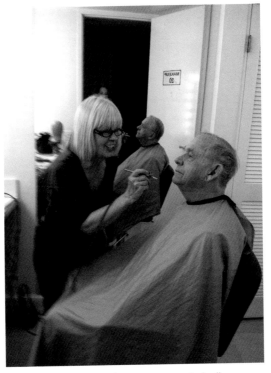

"Let me make you pretty, baby."
Dina Ousley and John in the make-up trailer—2011

A family affair.
Peggy and Mike—2012

Loving it!
Peggy and a Budweiser Clydesdale—2014

Okay, I'll talk!
John in *Don't Drink the Water*—2015

Read 2:02 PM

Mike. Your father left for Meals-on-Wheels in his old gray Scion like he always does. Five hours later he returned in a bright, cherry red, slightly used Scion - the kind of car you expect a sexy chick to get out of – not an 85-year-old with whistling hearing aids, a squeaky foot brace, and a groaning hernia. Counting my blessings. It's not a motorcycle. Mom

A man outstanding in a field of sunflowers.
John—2016

A new friend.
John and Beverly—2017

Hi Mike. We went to the state fair yesterday, and I rode a racehorse. It's been 25 years, but it felt like just yesterday! Dad always complained about veterinarian and farrier and feed bills, but fell in love with Old #2 and offered to buy him for me. Can you believe that? I rode for 15 minutes. This morning I could not walk! Thought I was dying. Fifteen lousy minutes. Eighty-one sucks!

Hi Mike. Dad hates shopping but came with me to mall this afternoon. We were separated, and when I finally found him in department store, he just said, "I'm a stranger in a strange land," like he was lost. Afterwards, as shoppers passed by, he whispered letters to me: "B" - "D" - "C" - "DD..." Funny man, your father. Childlike and innocent – sometimes. Enjoy the weekend. Mom

Phil and Pin Rowe—2011

Mike. Your father's hearing aids are worthless, and he's in denial. He accuses me of mumbling. I tell him it's because I'm hoarse from shouting. Neighbors are circulating a petition. They claim our TV's in violation of the Noise Control Act. Today I threatened to enroll us in a sign language class if Dad didn't have a hearing assessment. He did, and this afternoon a doctor removed half a pound of wax from his ears. Your father thinks you should auction it off for work scholarships. What do you think? Mom

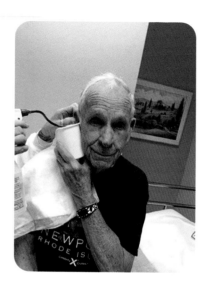

Dr. Lisa, miracle worker—2019

Mike. 20 days for me. 14 for your father. No volunteering, no walks, no church, no mah-jongg... We've gone through our rations. Down to one potato with roots longer than my hair, a shriveled onion, and a box of rice. Dr. says we'll survive, but will our marriage? Your father accused me of being addicted to ice cream! This, from a man who hides his ginger snaps under his recliner! I'm afraid he wants to kick me off the island. I know one thing: if I don't get a Big Mac soon, I won't be responsible for my actions!

Here's to us!
Scott, Mike, and Phil Rowe—2010